EVERYMAN,
I WILL GO WITH THEE
AND BE THY GUIDE,
IN THY MOST NEED
TO GO BY THY SIDE

EVERYMAN'S LIBRARY
POCKET POETS

BRONTË

POEMS

EVERYMAN'S LIBRARY
POCKET POETS

Alfred A. Knopf New York London Toronto

This selection by Peter Washington first published in
Everyman's Library, 1996
Copyright © 1996 by Everyman's Library

Thirteenth printing (US)

All rights reserved. Published in the United States by Alfred A. Knopf,
a division of Penguin Random House LLC, New York, and in Canada by
Penguin Random House Canada Limited, Toronto. Distributed by Penguin
Random House LLC, New York. Published in the United Kingdom by
Everyman's Library, 50 Albemarle Street, London W1S 4BD and
distributed by Penguin Random House UK,
20 Vauxhall Bridge Road, London SW1V 2SA.

www.randomhouse.com/everymans
www.everymanslibrary.co.uk

ISBN 978-0-679-44725-2 (US)
978-1-85715-728-4 (UK)

A CIP catalogue record for this book is available from the British Library

Typography by Peter B. Willberg

Typeset in the UK by AccComputing, North Barrow, Somerset

Printed and bound in Germany by GGP Media GmbH, Pössneck

CONTENTS

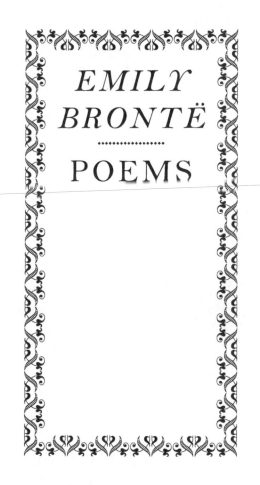

EMILY BRONTË

POEMS

POEMS

HIGH WAVING HEATHER

High waving heather 'neath stormy blasts bending
Midnight and moonlight and bright shining stars
Darkness and glory rejoicingly blending
Earth rising to heaven and heaven descending
Man's spirit away from its drear dungeon sending
Bursting the fetters and breaking the bars

All down the mountain sides wild forests lending
One mighty voice to the life giving wind
Rivers their banks in the jubilee rending
Fast through the valleys a reckless course wending
Wider and deeper their waters extending
Leaving a desolate desert behind

Shining and lowering and swelling and dying
Changing forever from midnight to noon
Roaring like thunder like soft music sighing
Shadows on shadows advancing and flying
Lightning bright flashes the deep gloom defying
Coming as swiftly and fading as soon

WILL THE DAY BE BRIGHT OR CLOUDY?

Will the day be bright or cloudy?
Sweetly has its dawn begun
But the heaven may shake with thunder
Ere the setting of the sun

Lady watch Apollo's journey
Thus thy first born's course shall be —
If his beams through summer vapours
Warm the earth all placidly
Her days shall pass like a pleasant dream in sweet
    tranquillity

If it darken if a shadow
Quench his rays and summon rain
Flowers may open buds may blossom
Bud and flower alike are vain
Her days shall pass like a mournful story in care and
    tears and pain

If the wind be fresh and free
The wide skies clear and cloudless blue
The woods and fields and golden flowers
Sparkling in sunshine and in dew
Her days shall pass in Glory's light the world's drear
    desert through

HOW STILL, HOW HAPPY!

How still, how happy! those are words
That once would scarce agree together
I loved the plashing of the surge –
The changing heaven the breezy weather,

More than smooth seas and cloudless skies
And solemn, soothing, softened airs
That in the forest woke no sighs
And from the green spray shook no tears

How still, how happy! now I feel
Where silence dwells is sweeter far
Than laughing mirth's most joyous swell
However pure its raptures are

Come sit down on this sunny stone
'Tis wintery light o'er flowerless moors –
But sit – for we are all alone
And clear expand heaven's breathless shores

I could think in the withered grass
Spring's budding wreaths we might discern
The violet's eye might shyly flash
And young leaves shoot among the fern

It is but thought – full many a night
The snow shall clothe those hills afar
And storms shall add a drearier blight
And winds shall wage a wilder war

Before the lark may herald in
Fresh foliage twined with blossoms fair
And summer days again begin
Their glory-haloed crown to wear

Yet my heart loves December's smile
As much as July's golden beam
Then let us sit and watch the while
The blue ice curdling on the stream –

HOW CLEAR SHE SHINES

How clear she shines! How quietly
    I lie beneath her guardian light;
While heaven and earth are whispering me,
    'Tomorrow, wake, but, dream tonight.'
Yes, Fancy, come, my Fairy love!
    These throbbing temples softly kiss;
And bend my lonely couch above
    And bring me rest, and bring me bliss.

The world is going, dark world, adieu!
    Grim world, conceal thee till the day;
The heart, thou canst not all subdue,
    Must still resist, if thou delay!

Thy love I will not, will not share;
    Thy hatred only wakes a smile;
Thy griefs may wound – thy wrongs may tear,
    But, oh, thy lies shall ne'er beguile!
While gazing on the stars that glow
    Above me, in that stormless sea,
I long to hope that all the woe
    Creation knows, is held in thee!

And this shall be my dream tonight;
    I'll think the heaven of glorious spheres
Is rolling on its course of light
    In endless bliss, through endless years;
I'll think, there's not one world above,
    Far as these straining eyes can see,
Where wisdom ever laughed at Love,
    Or Virtue crouched to Infamy;

Where, writhing 'neath the strokes of Fate,
    The mangled wretch was forced to smile;
To match his patience 'gainst her hate,
    His heart rebellious all the while.
Where Pleasure still will lead to wrong,
    And helpless Reason warn in vain;
And Truth is weak, and Treachery strong;
    And Joy the surest path to Pain;
And Peace, the lethargy of Grief;
    And Hope, a phantom of the soul;
And Life, a labour, void and brief;
    And Death, the despot of the whole!

STARS

Ah! why, because the dazzling sun
    Restored our Earth to joy,
Have you departed, every one,
    And left a desert sky?

All through the night, your glorious eyes
    Were gazing down in mine,
And with a full heart's thankful sighs,
    I blessed that watch divine.

I was at peace, and drank your beams
    As they were life to me;
And revelled in my changeful dreams,
    Like petrel on the sea.

Thought followed thought, star followed star,
    Through boundless regions, on;
While one sweet influence, near and far,
    Thrilled through, and proved us one!

Why did the morning dawn to break
    So great, so pure, a spell;
And scorch with fire, the tranquil cheek,
    Where your cool radiance fell?

Blood-red, he rose, and, arrow-straight,
    His fierce beams struck my brow;
The soul of nature, sprang, elate,
    But *mine* sank sad and low!

My lids closed down, yet through their veil,
    I saw him, blazing, still,
And steep in gold the misty dale,
    And flash upon the hill.

I turned me to the pillow, then,
    To call back night, and see
Your worlds of solemn light, again,
    Throb with my heart, and me!

It would not do – the pillow glowed,
    And glowed both roof and floor;
And birds sang loudly in the wood,
    And fresh winds shook the door;

The curtains waved, the wakened flies
    Were murmuring round my room,
Imprisoned there, till I should rise,
    And give them leave to roam.

Oh, stars, and dreams, and gentle night;
    Oh, night and stars return!
And hide me from the hostile light,
    That does not warm, but burn;

That drains the blood of suffering men;
    Drinks tears, instead of dew;
Let me sleep through his blinding reign,
    And only wake with you!

SHALL EARTH NO MORE INSPIRE THEE?

Shall Earth no more inspire thee,
Thou lonely dreamer now?
Since passion may not fire thee
Shall Nature cease to bow?

Thy mind is ever moving
In regions dark to thee;
Recall its useless roving –
Come back and dwell with me –

I know my mountain breezes
Enchant and soothe thee still –
I know my sunshine pleases
Despite thy wayward will –

When day with evening blending
Sinks from the summer sky,
I've seen thy spirit bending
In fond idolatry –

I've watched thee every hour —
I know my mighty sway —
I know my magic power
To drive thy griefs away —

Few hearts to mortals given
On earth so wildly pine
Yet none would ask a Heaven
More like this Earth than thine

Then let my winds caress thee —
Thy comrade let me be —
Since nought beside can bless thee
Return and dwell with me —

THE BLUE BELL IS
THE SWEETEST FLOWER

The blue bell is the sweetest flower
That waves in summer air
Its blossoms have the mightiest power
To soothe my spirit's care

There is a spell in purple heath
Too wildly, sadly drear
The violet has a fragrant breath
But fragrance will not cheer

The trees are bare, the sun is cold
And seldom, seldom seen –
The heavens have lost their zone of gold
The earth its robe of green

And ice upon the glancing stream
Has cast its sombre shade
And distant hills and valleys seem
In frozen mist arrayed –

The blue bell cannot charm me now
The heath has lost its bloom
The violets in the glen below
They yield no sweet perfume

But though I mourn the heather-bell
'Tis better far, away
I know how fast my tears would swell
To see it smile today

And that wood flower that hides so shy
Beneath the mossy stone
Its balmy scent and dewy eye
'Tis not for them I moan

It is the slight and stately stem
The blossom's silvery blue
The buds hid like a sapphire gem
In sheaths of emerald hue

'Tis these that breathe upon my heart
A calm and softening spell
That if it makes the tear-drop start
Has power to soothe as well

For these I weep, so long divided
Through winter's dreary day
In longing weep – but most when guided
On withered banks to stray

If chilly then the light should fall
Adown the dreary sky
And gild the dank and darkened wall
With transient brilliancy

How do I yearn, how do I pine
For the time of flowers to come
And turn me from that fading shine
To mourn the fields of home –

TO THE BLUE BELL

Sacred watcher, wave thy bells!
Fair hill flower and woodland child!
Dear to me in deep green dells –
Dearest on the mountains wild –

Blue bell, even as all divine
I have seen my darling shine –
Blue bell, even as wan and frail
I have seen my darling fail –
Thou hast found a voice for me –
And soothing words are breathed by thee –

Thus they murmur, 'Summer's sun
Warms me till my life is done –
Would I rather choose to die
Under winter's ruthless sky?

'Glad I bloom and calm I fade
Weeping twilight dews my bed
Mourner, mourner dry thy tears.
Sorrow comes with lengthened years!'

TELL ME TELL ME

Tell me tell me smiling child
What the past is like to thee?
An Autumn evening soft and mild
With a wind that sighs mournfully

Tell me what is the present hour?
A green and flowery spray
Where a young bird sits gathering its power
To mount and fly away

And what is the future happy one?
A sea beneath a cloudless sun
A mighty glorious dazzling sea
Stretching into infinity

WIND SINK TO REST

Wind sink to rest in the heather
Thy wild voice suits not me
I would have dreary weather
But all devoid of thee

Sun set from that evening heaven
Thy glad smile wins not mine
If light at all is given
O give me Cynthia's shine

ALL DAY I'VE TOILED

All day I've toiled but not with pain
In learning's golden mine
And now at eventide again
The moonbeams softly shine

There is no snow upon the ground
No frost on wind or wave
The south wind blew with gentlest sound
And broke their icy grave

'Tis sweet to wander here at night
To watch the winter die
With heart as summer sunshine light
And warm as summer's sky

O may I never lose the peace
That lulls me gently now
Though time should change my youthful face
And years should shade my brow

True to myself and true to all
May I be healthful still
And turn away from passion's call
And curb my own wild will

I KNOW NOT HOW IT FALLS ON ME

I know not how it falls on me
This summer evening, hushed and lone
Yet the faint wind comes soothingly
With something of an olden tone

Forgive me if I've shunned so long
Your gentle greeting earth and air
But sorrow withers even the strong
And who can fight against despair

WHAT USE IS IT TO SLUMBER HERE?

What use is it to slumber here:
Though the heart be sad and weary?
What use is it to slumber here
Though the day rise dark and dreary

For that mist may break when the sun is high
And this soul forget its sorrow
And the rosy ray of the closing day
May promise a brighter morrow

START NOT UPON THE MINSTER WALL

Start not upon the minster wall
Sunshine is shed in holy calm
And lonely though my footsteps fall
The saints shall shelter thee from harm

Shrink not if it be summer noon
This shadow should right welcome be
These stairs are steep but landed soon
We'll rest us long and quietly

What though our path be o'er the dead
They slumber soundly in the tomb
And why should mortals fear to tread
The pathway to their future home?

THE SUN HAS SET

The sun has set and the long grass now
Waves drearily in the evening wind
And the wild bird has flown from that old grey stone
In some warm nook a couch to find

In all the lonely landscape round
I see no sight and hear no sound
Except the wind that far away
Comes sighing o'er the heathy sea

HOW LOUD THE STORM SOUNDS

How loud the storm sounds round the Hall!
From arch to arch from door to door
Pillar and roof and granite wall
Rock like a cradle in its roar

That Elm tree by the haunted well
Greets no returning summer skies
Down with a rush the giant fell
And stretched athwart the path it lies

Hardly had passed the funeral train
So long delayed by wind and snow
And how they'll reach the house again
Tomorrow's dawn perhaps will show

IT WAS NIGHT

It was night and on the mountains
Fathoms deep the snow drifts lay
Streams and waterfalls and fountains
Down in darkness stole away

Long ago the hopeless peasant
Left his sheep all buried there
Sheep that through the summer pleasant
He had watched with fondest care

Now no more a cheerful ranger
Following pathways known of yore
Sad he stood a wildered stranger
On his own unbounded moor

MILD THE MIST UPON THE HILL

Mild the mist upon the hill
Telling not of storms tomorrow
No the day has wept its fill
Spent its store of silent sorrow

Oh I'm gone back to the days of youth
I am a child once more
And 'neath my father's sheltering roof
And near the old hall door

I watch this cloudy evening fall
After a day of rain
Blue mists sweet mists of summer pall
The horizon's mountain chain

The damp stands in the long green grass
As thick as morning's tears
And dreamy scents of fragrance pass
That breathe of other years

TO A WREATH OF SNOW

O transient voyager of heaven!
O silent sign of winter skies!
What adverse wind thy sail has driven
To dungeons where a prisoner lies?

Methinks the hands that shut the sun
So sternly from this mourning brow
Might still their rebel task have done
And checked a thing so frail as thou

They would have done it had they known
The talisman that dwelt in thee,
For all the suns that ever shone
Have never been so kind to me!

For many a week, and many a day
My heart was weighed with sinking gloom
When morning rose in mourning grey
And faintly lit my prison room,

But angel like, when I awoke,
Thy silvery form so soft and fair
Shining through darkness, sweetly spoke
Of cloudy skies and mountains bare

The dearest to a mountaineer
Who, all life long has loved the snow
That crowned her native summits drear,
Better, than greenest plains below —

And voiceless, soulless messenger
Thy presence waked a thrilling tone
That comforts me while thou art here
And will sustain when thou art gone

NO COWARD SOUL IS MINE

No coward soul is mine
No trembler in the world's storm-troubled sphere
I see Heaven's glories shine
And Faith shines equal arming me from Fear

O God within my breast
Almighty ever-present Deity
Life, that in me hast rest
As I Undying Life, have power in thee

Vain are the thousand creeds
That move men's hearts, unutterably vain,
Worthless as withered weeds
Or idlest froth amid the boundless main

To waken doubt in one
Holding so fast by thy infinity
So surely anchored on
The steadfast rock of Immortality

With wide-embracing love
Thy spirit animates eternal years
Pervades and broods above,
Changes, sustains, dissolves, creates and rears

Though Earth and moon were gone
And suns and universes ceased to be
And thou wert left alone
Every Existence would exist in thee

There is not room for Death
Nor atom that his might could render void
Since thou art Being and Breath
And what thou art may never be destroyed

IN THE EARTH, THE EARTH
THOU SHALT BE LAID

In the earth, the earth thou shalt be laid
A grey stone standing over thee;
Black mould beneath thee spread
And black mould to cover thee –

'Well, there is rest there
So fast come thy prophecy –
The time when my sunny hair
Shall with grass roots twined be'

But cold, cold is that resting place
Shut out from Joy and Liberty
And all who loved thy living face
Will shrink from its gloom and thee

'Not so, *here* the world is chill
And sworn friends fall from me
But *there*, they'll own me still
And prize my memory'

Farewell, then, all that love
All that deep sympathy:
Sleep on, heaven laughs above —
Earth never misses thee —

Turf-sod and tombstone drear
Part human company
One heart broke, only, there
That heart was worthy thee —

IT IS TOO LATE TO
CALL THEE NOW

It is too late to call thee now –
I will not nurse that dream again
For every joy that lit my brow
Would bring its after-storm of pain –

Besides the mist is half withdrawn,
The barren mountain-side lies bare
And sunshine and awaking morn
Paint no more golden visions there –

Yet ever in my grateful breast
Thy darling shade shall cherished be
For God alone doth know how blest
My early years have been in thee!

'TIS MOONLIGHT SUMMER MOONLIGHT

'Tis moonlight summer moonlight
All soft and still and fair
The solemn hour of midnight
Breathes sweet thoughts everywhere

But most where trees are sending
Their breezy boughs on high
Or stooping low are lending
A shelter from the sky

And there in those wild bowers
A lovely form is laid
Green grass and dew steeped flowers
Wave gently round her head

IF GRIEF FOR GRIEF
CAN TOUCH THEE

If grief for grief can touch thee,
If answering woe for woe,
If any ruth can melt thee
Come to me now!

I cannot be more lonely,
More drear I cannot be!
My worn heart throbs so wildly
'Twill break for thee –

And when the world despises –
When heaven repels my prayer –
Will not mine angel comfort?
Mine idol hear?

Yes by the tears I've poured,
By all my hours of pain
O I shall surely win thee
Beloved, again!

REMEMBRANCE

Cold in the earth – and the deep snow piled above thee,
Far, far, removed, cold in the dreary grave!
Have I forgot, my only Love, to love thee,
Severed at last by Time's all-severing wave?

Now, when alone, do my thoughts no longer hover
Over the mountains, on that northern shore,
Resting their wings where heath and fern-leaves cover
Thy noble heart for ever, ever more?

Cold in the earth – and fifteen wild Decembers,
From those brown hills, have melted into spring:
Faithful, indeed, is the spirit that remembers
After such years of change and suffering!

Sweet Love of youth, forgive, if I forget thee,
While the world's tide is bearing me along;
Other desires and other hopes beset me,
Hopes which obscure, but cannot do thee wrong!

No later light has lightened up my heaven,
No second morn has ever shone for me;
All my life's bliss from thy dear life was given,
All my life's bliss is in the grave with thee.

But, when the days of golden dreams had perished,
And even Despair was powerless to destroy;
Then did I learn how existence could be cherished,
Strengthened, and fed without the aid of joy.

Then did I check the tears of useless passion –
Weaned my young soul from yearning after thine;
Sternly denied its burning wish to hasten
Down to that tomb already more than mine.

And, even yet, I dare not let it languish,
Dare not indulge in memory's rapturous pain;
Once drinking deep of that divinest anguish,
How could I seek the empty world again?

SONG

The linnet in the rocky dells,
   The moor-lark in the air,
The bee among the heather bells,
   That hide my lady fair:

The wild deer browse above her breast;
   The wild birds raise their brood;
And they, her smiles of love caressed,
   Have left her solitude!

I ween, that when the grave's dark wall
   Did first her form retain;
They thought their hearts could ne'er recall
   The light of joy again.

They thought the tide of grief would flow
   Unchecked through future years;
But where is all their anguish now,
   And where are all their tears?

Well, let them fight for honour's breath,
   Or pleasure's shade pursue –
The dweller in the land of death
   Is changed and careless too.

And, if their eyes should watch and weep
　　Till sorrow's source were dry,
She would not, in her tranquil sleep,
　　Return a single sigh!

Blow, west-wind, by the lonely mound,
　　And murmur, summer-streams –
There is no need of other sound
　　To soothe my lady's dreams.

MAY FLOWERS ARE OPENING

May flowers are opening
And leaves unfolding free
There are bees in every blossom
And birds on every tree

The sun is gladly shining
The stream sings merrily
And I only am pining
And all is dark to me

O – cold cold is my heart
It will not cannot rise
It feels no sympathy
With those refulgent skies

Dead dead is my joy
I long to be at rest
I wish the damp earth covered
This desolate breast

If I were quite alone
It might not be so drear
When all hope was gone
At least I could not fear

But the glad eyes around me
Must weep as mine have done
And I must see the same gloom
Eclipse their morning sun

If heaven would rain on me
That future storm of care
So their fond hearts were free
I'd be content to bear

Alas as lightning withers
The young and aged tree
Both they and I shall fall beneath
The fate we cannot flee

STANZAS

I'll not weep that thou art going to leave me,
   There's nothing lovely here;
And doubly will the dark world grieve me,
   While thy heart suffers there.

I'll not weep, because the summer's glory
   Must always end in gloom;
And, follow out the happiest story –
   It closes with a tomb!

And I am weary of the anguish
   Increasing winters bear;
Weary to watch the spirit languish
   Through years of dead despair.

So, if a tear, when thou art dying,
   Should haply fall from me,
It is but that my soul is sighing,
   To go and rest with thee.

THE NIGHT-WIND

In summer's mellow midnight
A cloudless moon shone through
Our open parlour window
And rosetrees wet with dew

I sat in silent musing –
The soft wind waved my hair
It told me Heaven was glorious
And sleeping Earth was fair –

I needed not its breathing
To bring such thoughts to me
But still it whispered lowly
'How dark the woods will be! –

'The thick leaves in my murmur
Are rustling like a dream,
And all their myriad voices
Instinct with spirit seem'

I said, 'Go gentle singer,
Thy wooing voice is kind
But do not think its music
Has power to reach my mind –

'Play with the scented flower,
The young tree's supple bough –
And leave my human feelings
In their own course to flow'

The Wanderer would not leave me
Its kiss grew warmer still –
'O come,' it sighed so sweetly
'I'll win thee 'gainst thy will –

'Have we not been from childhood friends?
Have I not loved thee long?
As long as thou has loved the night
Whose silence wakes my song?

'And when thy heart is laid at rest
Beneath the church-yard stone
I shall have time enough to mourn
And thou to be alone' –

FAIR SINKS THE SUMMER EVENING

Fair sinks the summer evening now
In softened glory round my home;
The sky upon its holy brow
Wears not a cloud that speaks of gloom.

The old tower, shrined in golden light,
Looks down on the descending sun –
So gently evening blends with night
You scarce can say that day is done –

And this is just the joyous hour
When we were wont to burst away,
To 'scape from labour's tyrant power
And cheerfully go out to play –

Then why is all so sad and lone?
No merry foot-step on the stair –
No laugh – no heart-awaking tone
But voiceless silence everywhere –

I've wandered round our garden-ground
And still it seemed at every turn
That I should greet approaching feet
And words upon the breezes borne

In vain — they will not come today
And morning's beam will rise as drear
Then tell me — are they gone for aye
Our sun blinks through the mists of care?

Ah no, reproving Hope doth say
Departed joys 'tis fond to mourn
When every storm that hides their ray
Prepares a more divine return —

I AM THE ONLY BEING WHOSE DOOM

I am the only being whose doom
No tongue would ask no eye would mourn
I never caused a thought of gloom
A smile of joy since I was born

In secret pleasure – secret tears
This changeful life has slipped away
As friendless after eighteen years
As lone as on my natal day

There have been times I cannot hide
There have been times when this was drear
When my sad soul forgot its pride
And longed for one to love me here

But those were in the early glow
Of feelings not subdued by care
And they have died so long ago
I hardly now believe they were

First melted off the hope of youth
Then Fancy's rainbow fast withdrew
And then experience told me truth
In mortal bosoms never grew

'Twas grief enough to think mankind
All hollow servile insincere –
But worse to trust to my own mind
And find the same corruption there

A LITTLE WHILE, A LITTLE WHILE

A little while, a little while
The noisy crowd are barred away;
And I can sing and I can smile
A little while I've holiday!

Where wilt thou go my harassed heart?
Full many a land invites thee now;
And places near, and far apart
Have rest for thee, my weary brow –

There is a spot 'mid barren hills
Where winter howls and driving rain
But if the dreary tempest chills
There is a light that warms again

The house is old, the trees are bare
And moonless bends the misty dome
But what on earth is half so dear –
So longed for as the hearth of home?

The mute bird sitting on the stone,
The dank moss dripping from the wall,
The garden-walk with weeds o'ergrown
I love them – how I love them all!

Shall I go there? or shall I seek
Another clime, another sky.
Where tongues familiar music speak
In accents dear to memory?

Yes, as I mused, the naked room,
The flickering firelight died away
And from the midst of cheerless gloom
I passed to bright, unclouded day —

A little and a lone green lane
That opened on a common wide
A distant, dreamy, dim blue chain
Of mountains circling every side —

A heaven so clear, an earth so calm,
So sweet, so soft, so hushed an air
And, deepening still the dreamlike charm,
Wild moor-sheep feeding everywhere —

That was the scene — I knew it well
I knew the pathways far and near
That winding o'er each billowy swell
Marked out the tracks of wandering deer

Could I have lingered but an hour
It well had paid a week of toil
But truth has banished fancy's power
I hear my dungeon bars recoil –

Even as I stood with raptured eye
Absorbed in bliss so deep and dear
My hour of rest had fleeted by
And given me back to weary care –

DEATH

Death! that struck when I was most confiding
In my certain faith of joy to be –
Strike again, Time's withered branch dividing
From the fresh root of Eternity!

Leaves, upon Time's branch, were growing brightly,
Full of sap, and full of silver dew;
Birds beneath its shelter gathered nightly;
Daily round its flowers the wild bees flew,

Sorrow passed, and plucked the golden blossom;
Guilt stripped off the foliage in its pride;
But, within its parent's kindly bosom,
Flowered for ever Life's restoring tide.

Little mourned I for the parted gladness,
For the vacant nest and silent song –
Hope was there, and laughed me out of sadness;
Whispering, 'Winter will not linger long!'

And, behold! with tenfold increase blessing,
Spring adorned the beauty-burdened spray;
Wind and rain and fervent heat, caressing,
Lavished glory on that second May!

High it rose – no winged grief could sweep it;
Sin was scared to distance with its shine;
Love, and its own life, had power to keep it
From all wrong – from every blight but thine!

Cruel Death! The young leaves droop and languish;
Evening's gentle air may still restore –
No! the morning sunshine mocks my anguish –
Time, for me, must never blossom more!

Strike it down, that other boughs may flourish
Where that perished sapling used to be;
Thus, at least, its mouldering corpse will nourish
That from which it sprung – Eternity.

TO A.S. 1830

Where beams the sun the brightest
In the noons of sweet July?
Where falls the snow the lightest
From bleak December's sky?

Where can the weary lay his head
And lay it safe the while
In a grave that never shuts its dead
From heaven's benignant smile?

Upon the earth in sunlight
Spring grass grows green and fair
But beneath the earth is midnight –
Eternal midnight there!

Then why lament that those we love
Escape Earth's dungeon Tomb?
As if the flowers that blow above
Could charm its undergloom –

From morning's faintest dawning
Till evening's deepest shade
Thou wilt not cease thy mourning
To know where she is laid;

But if to weep above her grave
Be such a priceless boon
Go, shed thy tears in Ocean's wave
And they will reach it soon.

Yet midst thy wild repining
Mad though that anguish be
Think heaven on her is shining
Even as it shines on thee –

With thy mind's vision pierce the Deep
Look how she rests below
And tell me why such blessed sleep
Should cause such bitter woe?

YES HOLY BE THY RESTING PLACE

Yes holy be thy resting place
Wherever thou may'st lie
The sweetest winds breathe on thy face
The softest of the sky

And will not guardian Angels send
Kind dreams and thoughts of love
Though I no more may watchful bend
Thy longed repose above?

And will not heaven itself bestow
A beam of glory there
That summer's grass more green may grow
And summer's flowers more fair?

Farewell farewell 'tis hard to part
Yet loved one it must be
I would not rend another heart
Not even by blessing thee

Go we must break affection's chain
Forget the hopes of years
Nay grieve not willest thou remain
To waken wilder tears

This herald breeze with thee and me
Roved in the dawning day
And thou shouldest be where it shall be
Ere evening far away

A DEATH-SCENE

'O Day! he cannot die
When thou so fair art shining!
O Sun, in such a gorious sky,
So tranquilly declining;

'He cannot leave thee now,
While fresh west winds are blowing,
And all around his youthful brow
Thy cheerful light is glowing!

'Edward, awake, awake –
The golden evening gleams
Warm and bright on Arden's lake –
Arouse thee from thy dreams!

'Beside thee, on my knee,
My dearest friend! I pray
That thou, to cross the eternal sea,
Wouldst yet one hour delay:

'I hear its billows roar –
I see them foaming high;
But no glimpse of a further shore
Has blest my straining eye.

'Believe not what they urge
Of Eden isles beyond;
Turn back, from that tempestuous surge,
To thy own native land.

'It is not death, but pain
That struggles in thy breast –
Nay, rally, Edward, rouse again;
I cannot let thee rest!'

One long look, that sore reproved me
For the woe I could not bear –
One mute look of suffering moved me
To repent my useless prayer:

And, with sudden check, the heaving
Of distraction passed away;
Not a sign of further grieving
Stirred my soul that awful day.

Paled, at length, the sweet sun setting;
Sunk to peace the twilight breeze:
Summer dews fell softly, wetting
Glen, and glade, and silent trees.

Then his eyes began to weary,
Weighed beneath a mortal sleep;
And their orbs grew strangely dreary,
Clouded, even as they would weep.

But they wept not, but they changed not,
Never moved, and never closed;
Troubled still, and still they ranged not —
Wandered not, nor yet reposed!

So I knew that he was dying —
Stooped, and raised his languid head;
Felt no breath, and heard no sighing,
So I knew that he was dead.

LINES

I die but when the grave shall press
The heart so long endeared to thee
When earthly cares no more distress
And earthly joys are nought to me

Weep not, but think that I have past
Before thee o'er a sea of gloom
Have anchored safe and rest at last
Where tears and mourning cannot come

'Tis I should weep to leave thee here
On that dark Ocean sailing drear
With storms around and fears before
And no kind light to point the shore

But long or short though life may be
'Tis nothing to eternity
We part below to meet on high
Where blissful ages never die

WEANED FROM LIFE
AND TORN AWAY

Weaned from life and torn away
In the morning of thy day
Bound in everlasting gloom
Buried in a hopeless tomb

Yet upon thy bended knee
Thank the power banished thee
Chain and bar and dungeon wall
Saved thee from a deadlier thrall

Thank the power that made thee part
Ere that parting broke thy heart
Wildly rushed the mountain spring
From its source of fern and ling
How invincible its roar
Had its waters won the shore

THE PHILOSOPHER

'Enough of thought, philosopher!
    Too long hast thou been dreaming
Unenlightened, in this chamber drear,
    While summer's sun is beaming!
Space-sweeping soul, what sad refrain
Concludes thy musings once again?

    '"Oh, for the time when I shall sleep
    Without identity,
    And never care how rain may steep,
    Or snow may cover me!
    No promised heaven, these wild desires,
    Could all, or half fulfil;
    No threatened hell, with quenchless fires,
    Subdue this quenchless will!"'

'So said I, and still say the same;
    Still, to my death, will say –
Three gods, within this little frame,
    Are warring night and day;
Heaven could not hold them all, and yet
    They all are held in me;
And must be mine till I forget
    My present entity!

Oh, for the time, when in my breast
    Their struggles will be o'er!
Oh, for the day, when I shall rest,
    And never suffer more!'

'I saw a spirit, standing, man,
    Where thou doth stand – an hour ago,
And round his feet three rivers ran,
    Of equal depth, and equal flow –
A golden stream – and one like blood;
    And one like sapphire seemed to be;
But where they joined their triple flood
    It tumbled in an inky sea.

The spirit sent his dazzling gaze
    Down through that ocean's gloomy night
Then, kindling all, with sudden blaze,
    The glad deep sparkled wide and bright –
White as the sun, far, far more fair
    Than its divided sources were!'

'And even for that spirit, seer,
    I've watched and sought my life-time long;
Sought him in heaven, hell, earth, and air –
    An endless search, and always wrong!
Had I but seen his glorious eye
    Once light the clouds that wilder me,

I ne'er had raised this coward cry
    To cease to think, and cease to be;
I ne'er had called oblivion blest,
    Nor, stretching eager hands to death,
Implored to change for senseless rest
    This sentient soul, this living breath –
Oh, let me die – that power and will
    Their cruel strife may close;
And conquered good, and conquering ill
    Be lost in one repose!'

STANZAS TO —

Well, some may hate, and some may scorn,
And some may quite forget thy name;
But my sad heart must ever mourn
Thy ruined hopes, thy blighted fame!
'Twas thus I thought, an hour ago,
Even weeping o'er that wretch's woe;
One word turned back my gushing tears,
And lit my altered eye with sneers.
Then 'Bless the friendly dust,' I said,
'That hides thy unlamented head!
Vain as thou wert, and weak as vain,
The slave of Falsehood, Pride, and Pain, –
My heart has nought akin to thine;
Thy soul is powerless over mine.'

But these were thoughts that vanished too;
Unwise, unholy, and untrue:
Do I despise the timid deer,
Because his limbs are fleet with fear?
Or, would I mock the wolf's death-howl,
Because his form is gaunt and foul?
Or, hear with joy the leveret's cry,
Because it cannot bravely die?
No! Then above his memory
Let Pity's heart as tender be;
Say, 'Earth, lie lightly on that breast
And, kind Heaven, grant that spirit rest!'

LINES

Far away is the land of rest
Thousand miles are stretched between
Many a mountain's stormy crest
Many a desert void of green

Wasted worn is the traveller
Dark his heart and dim his eye
Without hope or comforter
Faltering faint and ready to die

Often he looks to the ruthless sky
Often he looks o'er his dreary road
Often he wishes down to lie
And render up life's tiresome load

But yet faint not mournful man
Leagues on leagues are left behind
Since your sunless course began
Then go on to toil resigned

If you still despair control
Hush its whispers in your breast
You shall reach the final goal
You shall win the land of rest

HARP OF WILD AND
DREAM LIKE STRAIN

Harp of wild and dream like strain
When I touch thy strings
Why dost thou repeat again
Long forgotten things?

Harp in other earlier days
I could sing to thee
And not one of all my lays
Vexed my memory

But now if I awake a note
That gave me joy before
Sounds of sorrow from thee float
Changing evermore

Yet still steeped in memory's dyes
They come sailing on
Darkening all my summer skies
Shutting out my sun

REDBREAST EARLY IN
THE MORNING

Redbreast early in the morning
Dark and cold and cloudy grey
Wildly tender is thy music
Chasing the angry thoughts away

*

My heart is not enraptured now
My eyes are full of tears
And constant sorrow on my brow
Has done the work of years

It was not hope that wrecked at once
The spirit's early storm
But a long life of solitude
Hopes quenched and rising thoughts subdued
A bleak November's calm

*

What woke it then? A little child
Strayed from its father's cottage door
And in the hour of moonlight mild
Laid lonely on the desert moor

*

I heard it then you heard it too
And seraph sweet it sang to you
But like the shriek of misery
That wild wild music wailed to me

HOPE

Hope was but a timid friend;
   She sat without the grated den,
Watching how my fate would tend,
   Even as selfish-hearted men.

She was cruel in her fear;
   Through the bars, one dreary day,
I looked out to see her there,
   And she turned her face away!

Like a false guard, false watch keeping,
   Still in strife, she whispered peace;
She would sing while I was weeping;
   If I listened, she would cease.

False she was, and unrelenting;
   When my last joys strewed the ground,
Even Sorrow saw, repenting,
   Those sad relics scattered round;

Hope, whose whisper would have given
   Balm to all my frenzied pain,
Stretched her wings, and soared to heaven,
   Went, and ne'er returned again!

SYMPATHY

There should be no despair for you
    While nightly stars are burning;
While evening pours its silent dew
    And sunshine gilds the morning.
There should be no despair – though tears
    May flow down like a river:
Are not the best beloved of years
    Around your heart for ever?

They weep, you weep, it must be so;
    Winds sigh as you are sighing,
And Winter sheds his grief in snow
    Where Autumn's leaves are lying:
Yet, these revive, and from their fate
    Your fate cannot be parted:
Then, journey on, if not elate,
    Still, *never* broken-hearted!

SONG

O between distress and pleasure
Fond affection cannot be
Wretched hearts in vain would treasure
Friendship's joys when others flee

Well I know thine eye would never
Smile while mine grieved willingly
Yet I know thine eye forever
Could not weep in sympathy

Let us part the time is over
When I thought and felt like thee
I will be an Ocean rover
I will sail the desert sea

Isles there are beyond its billow
Lands where woe may wander free
And beloved thy midnight pillow
Will be soft unwatched by me

Not on each returning morrow
When thy heart bounds ardently
Need'st thou then dissemble sorrow
Marking my despondency

Day by day some dreary token
Will forsake thy memory
Till at last all old links broken
I shall be a dream to thee

TO IMAGINATION

When weary with the long day's care,
    And earthly change from pain to pain,
And lost and ready to despair,
    Thy kind voice calls me back again:
Oh, my true friend! I am not lone,
While thou canst speak with such a tone!

So hopeless is the world without;
    The world within I doubly prize;
Thy world, where guile, and hate, and doubt,
    And cold suspicion never rise;
Where thou, and I, and Liberty,
Have undisputed sovereignty.

What matters it, that, all around,
    Danger, and guilt, and darkness lie,
If but within our bosom's bound
    We hold a bright, untroubled sky,
Warm with ten thousand mingled rays
Of suns that know no winter days?

Reason, indeed, may oft complain
    For Nature's sad reality,
And tell the suffering heart how vain
    Its cherished dreams must always be;
And Truth may rudely trample down
The flowers of Fancy, newly-blown:

But, thou art ever there, to bring
    The hovering vision back, and breathe
New glories o'er the blighted spring,
    And call a lovelier Life from Death,
And whisper, with a voice divine,
Of real worlds, as bright as thine.

I trust not to thy phantom bliss,
    Yet, still, in evening's quiet hour,
With never-failing thankfulness,
    I welcome thee, Benignant Power;
Sure solacer of human cares,
And sweeter hope, when hope despairs!

WHEN DAYS OF BEAUTY
DECK THE EARTH

When days of Beauty deck the earth
Or stormy nights descend
How well my spirit knows the path
On which it ought to wend

It seeks the consecrated spot
Beloved in childhood's years
The space between is all forgot
Its sufferings and its tears

O DREAM, WHERE ART THOU NOW?

O Dream, where art thou now?
Long years have past away
Since last, from off thine angel brow
I saw the light decay –

Alas, alas for me
Thou wert so bright and fair,
I could not think thy memory
Would yield me nought but care!

The sun-beam and the storm,
The summer-eve divine,
The silent night of solemn calm,
The full moon's cloudless shine

Were once entwined with thee
But now, with weary pain –
Lost vision! 'tis enough for me –
Thou canst not shine again –

MY COMFORTER

Well hast thou spoken, and yet, not taught
  A feeling strange or new;
Thou hast but roused a latent thought,
A cloud-closed beam of sunshine, brought
  To gleam in open view.

Deep down, concealed within my soul,
  That light lies hid from men;
Yet, glows unquenched – though shadows roll,
Its gentle ray cannot control,
  About the sullen den.

Was I not vexed, in these gloomy ways
  To walk alone so long?
Around me, wretches uttering praise,
Or howling o'er their hopeless days,
  And each with Frenzy's tongue; –

A brotherhood of misery,
  Their smiles as sad as sighs;
Whose madness daily maddened me,
Distorting into agony
  The bliss before my eyes!

So stood I, in Heaven's glorious sun,
    And in the glare of Hell;
My spirit drank a mingled tone,
Of seraph's song, and demon's moan;
What my soul bore, my soul alone
    Within itself may tell!

Like a soft air, above a sea,
    Tossed by the tempest's stir;
A thaw-wind, melting quietly
The snow-drift, on some wintry lea;
No: what sweet thing resembles thee,
    My thoughtful Comforter?

And yet a little longer speak,
    Calm this resentful mood;
And while the savage heart grows meek,
For other token do not seek,
But let the tear upon my cheek
    Evince my gratitude!

PLEAD FOR ME

Oh, thy bright eyes must answer now,
When Reason, with a scornful brow,
Is mocking at my overthrow!
Oh, thy sweet tongue must plead for me
And tell, why I have chosen thee!

Stern Reason is to judgment come,
Arrayed in all her forms of gloom:
Wilt thou, my advocate, be dumb?
No, radiant angel, speak and say,
Why I did cast the world away.

Why I have persevered to shun
The common paths that others run,
And on a strange road journeyed on,
Heedless, alike, of wealth and power –
Of glory's wreath and pleasure's flower.

These, once, indeed, seemed Beings Divine;
And they, perchance, heard vows of mine,
And saw my offerings on their shrine;
But, careless gifts are seldom prized,
And *mine* were worthily despised.

So, with a ready heart I swore
To seek their altar-stone no more;
And gave my spirit to adore
Thee, ever-present, phantom thing;
My slave, my comrade, and my king,

A slave, because I rule thee still;
Incline thee to my changeful will,
And make thy influence good or ill:
A comrade, for by day and night
Thou art my intimate delight, –

My darling pain that wounds and sears
And wrings a blessing out from tears
By deadening me to earthly cares;
And yet, a king, though Prudence well
Have taught thy subject to rebel.

And am I wrong to worship, where
Faith cannot doubt, nor hope despair,
Since my own soul can grant my prayer?
Speak, God of visions, plead for me,
And tell why I have chosen thee!

SELF-INTERROGATION

'The evening passes fast away,
    'Tis almost time to rest;
What thoughts has left the vanished day,
    What feelings, in thy breast?'

'The vanished day? It leaves a sense
    Of labour hardly done;
Of little, gained with vast expense, –
    A sense of grief alone!

'Time stands before the door of Death,
    Upbraiding bitterly;
And Conscience, with exhaustless breath,
    Pours black reproach on me:

'And though I've said that Conscience lies,
    And Time should Fate condemn;
Still, sad Repentance clouds my eyes,
    And makes me yield to them!'

'Then art thou glad to seek repose?
    Art glad to leave the sea,
And anchor all thy weary woes
    In calm Eternity?

'Nothing regrets to see thee go –
    Not one voice sobs "farewell",
And where thy heart has suffered so,
    Canst thou desire to dwell?'

'Alas! The countless links are strong
    That bind us to our clay;
The loving spirit lingers long,
    And would not pass away!

'And rest is sweet, when laurelled fame
    Will crown the soldier's crest;
But, a brave heart, with a tarnished name,
    Would rather fight than rest.'

'Well, thou hast fought for many a year,
    Hast fought thy whole life through,
Hast humbled Falsehood, trampled Fear;
    What is there left to do?'

''Tis true, this arm has hotly striven,
    Has dared what few would dare;
Much have I done, and freely given,
    But little learnt to bear!'

'Look on the grave, where thou must sleep,
   Thy last, and strongest foe;
It is endurance not to weep,
   If that repose seem woe.

'The long war closing in defeat,
   Defeat serenely borne,
Thy midnight rest may still be sweet,
   And break in glorious morn!'

THE OLD STOIC

Riches I hold in light esteem;
  And Love I laugh to scorn;
And lust of fame was but a dream
  That vanished with the morn:

And if I pray, the only prayer
  That moves my lips for me
Is, 'Leave the heart that now I bear,
  And give me liberty!'

Yes, as my swift days near their goal,
  'Tis all that I implore;
In life and death, a chainless soul,
  With courage to endure.

LONG NEGLECT HAS WORN AWAY

Long neglect has worn away
Half the sweet enchanting smile
Time has turned the bloom to grey
Mould and damp the face defile

But that lock of silky hair
Still beneath the picture twined
Tells what once those features were
Paints their image on the mind

Fair the hand that traced that line
'Dearest ever deem me true'
Swiftly flew the fingers fine
When the pen that motto drew

SLEEP BRINGS NO JOY
TO ME

Sleep brings no joy to me
Remembrance never dies
My soul is given to misery
And lives in sighs

Sleep brings no rest to me
The shadows of the dead
My waking eyes may never see
Surround my bed

Sleep brings no hope to me
In soundest sleep they come
And with their doleful imagery
Deepen the gloom

Sleep brings no strength to me
No power renewed to brave
I only sail a wilder sea
A darker wave

Sleep brings no friend to me
To soothe and aid to bear
They all gaze on how scornfully
And I despair

Sleep brings no wish to knit
My harassed heart beneath
My only wish is to forget
In the sleep of death

AND LIKE MYSELF
LONE WHOLLY LONE

And like myself lone wholly lone
It sees the day's long sunshine glow
And like myself it makes its moan
In unexhausted woe

Give we the hills our equal prayer
Earth's breezy hills and heaven's blue sea
We ask for nothing further here
But our own hearts and liberty

Ah could my hand unlock its chain
How gladly would I watch it soar
And ne'er regret and ne'er complain
To see its shining eyes no more

But let me think that if today
It pines in cold captivity
Tomorrow both shall soar away
Eternally entirely Free

A.E. AND R.C.

Heavy hangs the raindrop
From the burdened spray;
Heavy broods the damp mist
On Uplands far away;

Heavy looms the dull sky,
Heavy rolls the sea –
And heavy beats the young heart
Beneath that lonely tree –

Never has a blue streak
Cleft the clouds since morn –
Never has his grim Fate
Smiled since he was born –

Frowning on the infant,
Shadowing childhood's joy,
Guardian angel knows not
That melancholy boy –

Day is passing swiftly
Its sad and sombre prime;
Youth is fast invading
Sterner manhood's time –

All the flowers are praying
For sun before they close
And he prays too, unknowing,
That sunless human rose!

Blossoms, that the west wind
Has never wooed to blow
Scentless are your petals
Your dew as cold as snow.

Soul, where kindred kindness
No early promise woke
Barren is your beauty
As weed upon the rock –

Wither, Brothers, wither,
You were vainly given –
Earth reserves no blessing
For the unblessed of Heaven!

Child of Delight! with sunbright hair
And seablue seadeep eyes
Spirit of Bliss, what brings thee here
Beneath these sullen skies?

Thou shouldest live in eternal spring
Where endless day is never dim
Why, seraph, has thy erring wing
Borne thee down to weep with him?

'Ah, not from heaven am I descended
And I do not come to mingle tears
But sweet is day, though with shadows blended
And though clouded, sweet are youthful years –

'I, the image of light and gladness
Saw and pitied that mournful boy
And I swore to take his gloomy sadness
And give to him my beamy joy –

'Heavy and dark the night is closing
Heavy and dark may its biding be
Better for all from grief reposing
And better for all who watch like me –

'Guardian angel, he lacks no longer;
Evil fortune he need not fear:
Fate is strong but Love is stronger
And more unsleeping than angel's care' –

FAITH AND DESPONDENCY

'The winter wind is loud and wild,
Come close to me, my darling child;
Forsake thy books, and mateless play;
And, while the night is gathering grey,
We'll talk its pensive hours away; —

'Iernë, round our sheltered hall
November's gusts unheeded call;
Not one faint breath can enter here
Enough to wave my daughter's hair,
And I am glad to watch the blaze
Glance from her eyes, with mimic rays;
To feel her cheek so softly pressed,
In happy quiet on my breast.

'But, yet, even this tranquillity
Brings bitter, restless thoughts to me;
And, in the red fire's cheerful glow,
I think of deep glens, blocked with snow;
I dream of moor, and misty hill,
Where evening closes dark and chill;
For, lone, among the mountains cold,
Lie those that I have loved of old.
And my heart aches, in hopeless pain
Exhausted with repinings vain,
That I shall greet them ne'er again!'

'Father, in early infancy,
When you were far beyond the sea,
Such thoughts were tyrants over me!
I often sat, for hours together,
Through the long nights of angry weather,
Raised on my pillow, to descry
The dim moon struggling in the sky;
Or, with strained ear, to catch the shock,
Of rock with wave, and wave with rock;
So would I fearful vigil keep,
And, all for listening, never sleep.
But this world's life has much to dread,
Not so, my Father, with the dead.

    'Oh! not for them, should we despair,
The grave is drear, but they are not there;
Their dust is mingled with the sod,
Their happy souls are gone to God!
You told me this, and yet you sigh,
And murmur that your friends must die.
Ah! my dear father, tell me why?
For, if your former words were true,
How useless would such sorrow be;
As wise, to mourn the seed which grew
Unnoticed on its parent tree,
Because it fell in fertile earth,
And sprang up to a glorious birth –

Struck deep its root, and lifted high
Its green boughs, in the breezy sky.

'But, I'll not fear, I will not weep
For those whose bodies rest in sleep, –
I know there is a blessed shore,
    Opening its ports for me, and mine;
And, gazing Time's wide waters o'er,
    I weary for that land divine,
Where we were born, where you and I
Shall meet our Dearest, when we die;
From suffering and corruption free,
Restored into the Deity.'

'Well hast thou spoken, sweet, trustful child!
    And wiser than thy sire;
And worldly tempests, raging wild,
    Shall strengthen thy desire –
Thy fervent hope, through storm and foam,
    Through wind and ocean's roar,
To reach, at last, the eternal home,
    The steadfast, changeless, shore!'

THE NIGHT WAS DARK
YET WINTER BREATHED

The night was dark yet winter breathed
With softened sighs on Gondal's shore
And though its wind repining grieved
It chained the snow swollen streams no more

How deep into the wilderness
My horse had strayed, I cannot say
But neither morsel nor caress
Would urge him farther on the way

So loosening from his neck the rein
I set my worn companion free
And billowy hill and boundless plain
Full soon divided him from me

The sullen clouds lay all unbroken
And blackening round the horizon drear
But still they gave no certain token
Of heavy rain or tempests near

I paused confounded and distressed
Down in the heath my limbs I threw
Yet wilder as I longed for rest
More wakeful heart and eyelids grew

It was about the middle night
And under such a starless dome
When gliding from the mountain's height
I saw a shadowy spirit come

Her wavy hair on her shoulders bare
It shone like soft clouds round the moon
Her noiseless feet like melting sleet
Gleamed white a moment then were gone

'What seek you now on this bleak moor's brow
Where wanders that form from heaven descending?'
It was thus I said as her graceful head
The spirit above my couch was bending

'This is my home where whirlwinds blow
Where snowdrifts round my path are swelling
'Tis many a year 'tis long ago
Since I beheld another dwelling

'When thick and fast the smothering blast
O'erwhelmed the hunter on the plain
If my cheek grew pale in its loudest gale
May I never tread the hills again

'The shepherd had died on the mountainside
But my ready aid was near him then
I led him back o'er the hidden track
And gave him to his native glen

'When tempests roar on the lonely shore
I light my beacon with sea-weeds dry
And it flings its fire through the darkness dire
And gladdens the sailor's hopeless eye

'And the scattered sheep I love to keep
Their timid forms to guard from harm
I have a spell and they know it well
And I save them with a powerful charm

'Thy own good steed on his friendless bed
A few hours since you left to die
But I knelt by his side and the saddle untied
And life returned to his glazing eye

'And deem thou not that quite forgot
My mercy will forsake me now
I bring thee care and not Despair
Abasement but not overthrow

'To a silent home thy foot may come
And years may follow of toilsome pain
But yet I swear by that Burning Tear
The loved shall meet on its hearth again'

THE STARRY NIGHT
SHALL TIDINGS BRING

The starry night shall tidings bring
Go out upon the breezy moor
Watch for a bird with sable wing
And beak and talons dripping gore

Look not around look not beneath
But mutely trace its airy way
Mark where it lights upon the heath
Then wanderer kneel thee down and pray

What fortune may await thee there
I will not and I dare not tell
But Heaven is moved by fervent prayer
And God is mercy – fare thee well!

ANTICIPATION

How beautiful the earth is still,
To thee – how full of happiness!
How little fraught with real ill,
Or unreal phantoms of distress!
How spring can bring thee glory, yet,
And summer win thee to forget
December's sullen time!
Why dost thou hold the treasure fast,
Of youth's delight, when youth is past,
    And thou art near thy prime?

When those who were thy own compeers,
Equals in fortune and in years,
Have seen their morning melt in tears,
    To clouded, smileless day;
Blest, had they died untried and young,
Before their hearts went wandering wrong,
Poor slaves, subdued by passions strong,
    A weak and helpless prey!

'Because, I hoped while they enjoyed,
And, by fulfilment, hope destroyed;
As children hope, with trustful breast,
I waited bliss – and cherished rest.
A thoughtful spirit taught me, soon,
That we must long till life be done;
That every phase of earthly joy
Must always fade, and always cloy:

'This I foresaw – and would not chase
   The fleeting treacheries;
But, with firm foot and tranquil face,
Held backward from that tempting race,
Gazed o'er the sands the waves efface,
   To the enduring seas –
There cast my anchor of desire
Deep in unknown eternity;
Nor ever let my spirit tire,
With looking for *what is to be!*

'It is hope's spell that glorifies,
Like youth, to my maturer eyes,
All Nature's million mysteries,
    The fearful and the fair –
Hope soothes me in the griefs I know;
She lulls my pain for others' woe,
And makes me strong to undergo
    What I am born to bear.

'Glad comforter! will I not brave,
Unawed, the darkness of the grave?
Nay, smile to hear Death's billows rave –
    Sustained, my guide, by thee?
The more unjust seems present fate,
The more my spirit swells elate,
Strong, in thy strength, to anticipate
    Rewarding destiny!'

HONOUR'S MARTYR

The moon is full this winter night;
　　The stars are clear, though few;
And every window glistens bright,
　　With leaves of frozen dew.

The sweet moon through your lattice gleams
　　And lights your room like day;
And there you pass, in happy dreams,
　　The peaceful hours away!

While I, with effort hardly quelling
　　The anguish in my breast,
Wander about the silent dwelling,
　　And cannot think of rest.

The old clock in the gloomy hall
　　Ticks on, from hour to hour;
And every time its measured call
　　Seems lingering slow and slower:

And oh, how slow that keen-eyed star
　　Has tracked the chilly grey!
What, watching yet! how very far
　　The morning lies away!

Without your chamber door I stand;
  Love, are you slumbering still?
My cold heart, underneath my hand,
  Has almost ceased to thrill.

Bleak, bleak the east wind sobs and sighs,
  And drowns the turret bell,
Whose sad note, undistinguished, dies
  Unheard, like my farewell!

Tomorrow, Scorn will blight my name,
  And Hate will trample me,
Will load me with a coward's shame –
  A traitor's perjury.

False friends will launch their covert sneers;
  True friends will wish me dead;
And I shall cause the bitterest tears
  That you have ever shed.

The dark deeds of my outlawed race
  Will then like virtues shine;
And men will pardon their disgrace,
  Beside the guilt of mine.

For, who forgives the accursed crime
    Of dastard treachery?
Rebellion, in its chosen time,
    May Freedom's champion be;

Revenge may stain a righteous sword,
    It may be just to slay;
But, traitor, traitor, – from *that* word
    All true breasts shrink away!

Oh, I would give my heart to death,
    To keep my honour fair;
Yet, I'll not give my inward faith
    My honour's *name* to spare!

Not even to keep your priceless love,
    Dare I, Beloved, deceive;
This treason should the future prove,
    Then, only then, believe!

I know the path I ought to go;
    I follow fearlessly,
Inquiring not what deeper woe
    Stern duty stores for me.

So foes pursue, and cold allies
    Mistrust me, every one:
Let me be false in others' eyes,
    If faithful in my own.

GERALDINE

'Twas night, her comrades gathered all
Within their city's rocky wall;
When flowers were closed and day was o'er
Their joyous hearts awoke the more

But lonely in her distant cave
She heard the river's restless wave
Chafing its banks with dreamy flow
Music for mirth, and wail for woe —

Palm trees and cedars towering high
Deepened the gloom of evening's sky
And thick did raven ringlets veil
Her forehead, drooped like lily pale

Yet I could hear my lady sing;
I knew she did not mourn,
For never yet from sorrow's spring
Such witching notes were born

Thus poured she in that cavern wild
The voice of feelings warm
As, bending o'er her beauteous child
She clasped its sleeping form —

'Why sank so soon the summer sun
From our Zedora's skies?
I was not tired, my darling one,
Of gazing in thine eyes –

'Methought the heaven whence thou hast come
Was lingering there awhile
And Earth seemed such an alien home
They did not dare to smile.

'Methought each moment something strange
Within their circles shone
And yet, through every magic change
They were Brenzaida's own.

'Methought – what thought I not, sweet love?
My whole heart centred there;
I breathed not but to send above
One gush of ardent prayer.

'Bless it, my gracious God, I cried,
Preserve thy mortal shrine
For thine own sake, be thou its guide
And keep it still divine!

'Say, sin shall never blanch that cheek
Nor suffering charge that brow
Speak, in thy mercy maker, speak
And seal it safe from woe!

'Why did I doubt? In God's control
Our mutual fates remain
And pure as now, my angel's soul
Must go to heaven again!'

The revellers in the city slept
My lady, in her woodland bed,
I, watching o'er her slumber wept
As one who mourns the dead!

THROUGH THE HOURS
OF YESTERNIGHT

Through the hours of yesternight
Hall and gallery blazed with light
Every lamp its lustre showered
On the adorer and the adored
None were sad that entered there
All were loved and all were fair
Some were dazzling like the sun
Shining down at summer noon
Some were sweet as amber even
Living in the depth of heaven
Some were soft and kind and gay
Morning's face not more divine
Some were like Diana's day
Midnight moonlight's holy shine

THE NIGHT IS DARKENING
ROUND ME

The night is darkening round me
The wild winds coldly blow
But a tyrant spell has bound me
And I cannot cannot go

The giant trees are bending
Their bare boughs weighed with snow
And the storm is fast descending
And yet I cannot go

Clouds beyond clouds above me
Wastes beyond wastes below
But nothing drear can move me
I will not cannot go

*

I'll come when thou art saddest
Laid alone in the darkened room
When the mad day's mirth has vanished
And the smile of joy is banished
From evening's chilly gloom

I'll come when the heart's real feeling
Has entire unbiased sway
And my influence o'er thee stealing
Grief deepening joy congealing
Shall bear thy soul away

Listen 'tis just the hour
The awful time for thee
Dost thou not feel upon thy soul
A flood of strange sensations roll
Forerunners of a sterner power
Heralds of me

*

I would have touched the heavenly key
That spoke alike of bliss and thee
I would have woke the entrancing song
But its words died upon my tongue
And then I knew that hallowed strain
Could never speak of joy again
And then I felt

COME HITHER CHILD

Come hither child – who gifted thee
With power to touch that string so well?
How daredst thou rouse up thoughts in me
Thoughts that I would – but cannot quell?

Nay chide not lady long ago
I heard those notes in Ula's hall
And had I known they'd waken woe
I'd weep their music to recall

But thus it was one festal night
When I was hardly six years old
I stole away from crowds and light
And sought a chamber dark and cold

I had no one to love me there
I knew no comrade and no friend
And so I went to sorrow where
Heaven only heaven saw me bend

Loud blew the wind 'twas sad to stay
From all that splendour barred away
I imaged in the lonely room
A thousand forms of fearful gloom

And with my wet eyes raised on high
I prayed to God that I might die
Suddenly in that silence drear
A sound of music reached my ear

And then a note I hear it yet
So full of soul so deeply sweet
I thought that Gabriel's self had come
To take me to my father's home

Three times it rose that seraph-strain
Then died nor lived ever again
But still the words and still the tone
Swell round my heart when all alone

LINES

The soft unclouded blue of air
The earth as golden-green and fair
And bright as Eden's used to be
That air and earth have rested me

Laid on the grass I lapsed away
Sank back again to childhood's day
All harsh thoughts perished memory mild
Subdued both grief and passion wild

But did the sunshine even now
That bathed his stern and swarthy brow
Oh did it wake I long to know
One whisper one sweet dream in him
One lingering joy that years ago
Had faded – lost in distance dim
That iron man was born like me
And he was once an ardent boy
He must have felt in infancy
The glory of a summer sky

Though storms untold his mind have tossed
He cannot utterly have lost
Remembrance of his early home
So lost that not a gleam may come

No vision of his mother's face
When she so fondly would set free
Her darling child from her embrace
To roam till eve at liberty –

Nor of his haunts nor of the flowers
His tiny hand would grateful bear
Returning from the darkening bowers
To weave into her glossy hair

I saw the light breeze kiss his cheek
His fingers 'mid the roses twined
I watched to mark one transient streak
Of pensive softness shade his mind

The open window showed around
A glowing park and glorious sky
And thick woods swelling with the sound
Of Nature's mingled harmony

Silent he sat. That stormy breast
At length, I said has deigned to rest
At length above that spirit flows
The waveless ocean of repose

Let me draw near 'twill soothe to view
His dark eyes dimmed with holy dew
Remorse even now may wake within
And half unchain his soul from sin

Perhaps this is the destined hour
When hell shall lose its fatal power
And heaven itself shall bend above
To hail the soul redeemed by love

Unmarked I gazed my idle thought
Panned with the ray whence shine it caught
One glance revealed how little care
He felt for all the beauty there

Oh crime can make the heart grow old
Sooner than years of wearing woe
Can turn the warmest bosom cold
As winter wind or polar snow

SLEEP NOT DREAM
NOT THIS BRIGHT DAY

Sleep not dream not this bright day
Will not cannot last for aye
Bliss like thine is bought by years
Dark with torment and with tears

Sweeter far than placid pleasure
Purer higher beyond measure
Yet alas the sooner turning
Into hopeless endless mourning

I love thee boy for all divine
All full of God thy features shine
Darling enthusiast holy child
Too good for this world's warring wild
Too heavenly now but doomed to be
Hell-like in heart and misery

And what shall change that angel brow
And quench that spirit's glorious glow
Relentless laws that disallow
True virtue and true joy below

And blame me not if when the dread
Of suffering clouds thy youthful head
If when by crime and sorrow tost
Thy wandering bark is wrecked and lost

I too depart I too decline
And make thy path no longer mine
'Tis thus that human minds will turn
All down and little to him and mourn
Yet all with long gaze fixed afar
Adoring virtue's distant star

THE BATTLE HAD PASSED
FROM THE HEIGHT

The battle had passed from the height
And still did evening fall
While heaven with its hosts of night
Gloriously canopied all

The dead around were sleeping
On heath and granite grey
And the dying their last watch were keeping
In the closing of the day

*

How golden bright from earth and heaven
The summer day declines
How gloriously o'er land and sea
The parting sunbeam shines

There is a voice in the wind that waves
Those bright rejoicing trees

*

Not a vapour had stained the breezeless blue
Not a cloud had dimmed the sun
From the time of morning's earliest dew
Till the summer day was done

And all as pure and all as bright
The beam of evening died
And purer still its parting light
Shone in Lake Elnor's tide

Waveless and calm lies that silent deep
In its wilderness of moors
Solemn and soft the moonbeams sleep
Upon its lengthy shores

The deer are gathered to their rest
The wild sheep seek the fold

       *

Only some spires of bright green grass
Transparently in sunshine quivering

A.G.A. TO A.E.

Lord of Elbë, on Elbë hill
The mist is thick and the wind is chill
And the heart of thy Friend from the dawn of day
Has sighed for sorrow that thou went away –

Lord of Elbë, how pleasant to me
The sound of thy blithesome step would be
Rustling the heath that, only now
Waves as the night-gusts over it blow

Bright are the fires in thy lonely home
I see them far off, and as deepens the gloom
Gleaming like stars through the high forest-boughs
Gladder they glow in the park's repose –

O Alexander! when I return,
Warm as those hearths my heart would burn,
Light as thine own, my foot would fall
If I might hear thy voice in the hall –

But thou art now on a desolate sea –
Parted from Gondal and parted from me –
All my repining is hopeless and vain,
Death never yields back his victims again –

WRITTEN ON RETURNING TO THE P. OF I. ON THE 10TH OF JANUARY 1827

The busy day has hurried by
And hearts greet kindred hearts once more
And swift the evening hours should fly
But what turns every gleaming eye
So often to the door?

And then so quick away – and why
Does sudden silence chill the round?
And laughter sink into a sigh –
And merry words to whispers die –
And gladness change to gloom?

O we are listening for a sound
We know shall ne'er be heard again
Sweet voices in the halls resound;
Fair forms, fond faces gather round
But all in vain – in vain!

Their feet shall never waken more
The echoes in these galleries wide,
Nor dare the snow on the mountain's brow,
Nor skim the river's frozen flow,
Nor wander down its side –

They who have been our life – our soul –
Through summer-youth, from childhood's spring –
Who bound us in one vigorous whole
To stand 'gainst Tyranny's control
For ever triumphing –

Who bore the brunt of battle's fray
The first to fight, the last to fall
Whose mighty minds – with kindred ray
Still led the van in Glory's way –
The idol chiefs of all –

They, they are gone! not for a while
As golden suns at night decline
And even in death our grief beguile
Foretelling, with a rose-red smile
How bright the morn will shine –

No these dark towers are lone and lorn;
This very crowd is vacancy;
And we must watch and wait and mourn
And half look out for their return;
And think their forms we see –

And fancy music in our ear
Such as their lips could only pour
And think we feel their presence near
And start to find they are not here
And never shall be more!

ROSINA

Weeks of wild delirium past –
Weeks of fevered pain,
Rest from suffering comes at last –
Reason dawns again –

It was a pleasant April day
Declining to the afternoon
Sunshine upon her pillow lay
As warm as middle June.

It told her how unconsciously
Early spring had hurried by
'Ah Time has not delayed for me!'
She murmured with a sigh.

'Angora's hills have heard their tread
The crimson flag is planted there –
Elderno's waves are rolling red,
While *I* lie fettered here?

'Nay, rather, Gondal's shaken throne
Is now secure and free;
And my King Julius reigns alone,
Debtless, alas! to me!'

Loud was the sudden gush of woe
From those who watched around;
Rosina turned, and sought to know
Why burst that boding sound.

'What then, my dreams are false,' she said
'Come maidens, answer me
Has Almedore in battle fled?
Have slaves subdued the free?

'I know it all, he could not bear
To leave me dying far away –
He fondly, madly lingered here
And we have lost the day!

'But check those coward sobs, and bring
My robes and smooth my tangled hair:
A noble victory you shall sing
For every hour's despair!

'When will he come? 'Twill soon be night –
He'll come when evening falls –
Oh I shall weary for the light
To leave my lonely halls!'

She turned her pallid face aside
As she would seek repose;
But dark Ambition's thwarted pride
Forbade her lids to close –

And still on all who waited by
Oppressive mystery hung;
And swollen with grief was every eye
And chained was every tongue.

They whispered nought, but, 'Lady, sleep,
Dear Lady, slumber now!
Had we not bitter cause to weep
While you were laid so low?

'And Hope can hardly deck the cheek
With sudden signs of cheer
When it has worn through many a week
The stamp of anguish drear' –

Fierce grew Rosina's gloomy gaze;
She cried, 'Dissemblers, own,
Exina's arms in victory blaze
Brenzaida's crest is down'

'Well, since it must be told, Lady,
Brenzaida's crest *is* down
Brenzaida's sun is set, Lady,
His empire overthrown!

'He died beneath this palace dome –
True hearts on every side –
Among his guards, within his home
Our glorious monarch died

'I saw him fall, I saw the gore
From his heart's fountain swell
And mingling on the marble floor
His murderer's life-blood fell –

'And now, 'mid northern mountains lone
His desert grave is made;
And, Lady, of your love, alone
Remains a mortal shade!'

THE WIDE CATHEDRAL AISLES ARE LONE

The wide cathedral Aisles are lone
The vast crowds vanished every one
There can be nought beneath that dome
But the cold tenants of the tomb

O look again for still on high
The lamps are burning gloriously
And look again for still beneath
A thousand thousand live and breathe

All mute as death regard the shrine
That gleams in lustre so divine
Where Gondal's monarchs bending low
After the hush of silent prayer
Take in heaven's sight their awful vow
And never dying union swear
King Julius lifts his impious eye
From the dark marble to the sky
Blasts with that Oath his perjured soul
And changeless is his cheek the while
Though burning thoughts that spurn control
Kindle a short and bitter smile
As face to face the kinsmen stand
His false hand clasped in Gerald's hand

WHERE WERE YE ALL?

Where were ye all? and where wert thou
I saw an eye that shone like thine
But dark curls waved around his brow
And his stern glance was strange to mine

And yet a dreamlike comfort came
Into my heart and anxious eye
And trembling yet to hear his name
I bent to listen watchfully

His voice though never heard before
Still spoke to me of years gone by
It seemed a vision to restore
That brought the hot tears to my eye

A.G.A. TO A.S.

At such a time, in such a spot
The world seems made of light
Our blissful hearts remember not
How surely follows night —

I cannot, Alfred, dream of aught
That casts a shade of woe;
That heaven is reigning in my thought
Which wood and wave and earth have caught
From skies that overflow —

That heaven which my sweet lover's brow
Has won me to adore —
Which from his blue eyes beaming now
Reflects a still intenser glow
Than nature's heaven can pour —

I know our souls are all divine
I know that when we die
What seems the vilest, even like thine
A part of God himself shall shine
In perfect purity —

But coldly breaks November's day
Its changes charmless all
Unmarked, unloved, they pass away
We do not wish one hour to stay
Nor sigh at evening's fall

And glorious is the gladsome rise
Of June's rejoicing morn
And who with unregretful eyes
Can watch the lustre leave its skies
To twilight's shade forlorn?

Then art thou not my golden June,
All mist and tempest free?
As shines earth's sun in summer noon
So heaven's sun shines in thee —

Let others seek its beams divine
In cell and cloister drear
But I have found a fairer shrine
And happier worship here —

By dismal rites they win their bliss
By penance, fasts, and fears —
I have one rite — a gentle kiss —
One penance — tender tears —

O could it thus forever be
That I might so adore
I'd ask for all eternity
To make a paradise for me,
My love – and nothing more!

SONG BY JULIUS ANGORA

Awake! awake! how loud the stormy morning
Calls up to life the nations resting round;
Arise, Arise, is it the voice of mourning
That breaks our slumber with so wild a sound?

The voice of mourning? Listen to its pealing;
That shout of triumph drowns the sigh of woe;
Each tortured heart forgets its wonted feeling,
Each faded cheek resumes its long-lost glow –

Our souls are full of gladness, God has given
Our arms to victory, our foes to death;
The crimson ensign waves its sheet in heaven –
The sea-green Standard lies in dust beneath.

Patriots, no stain is on your country's glory
Soldiers, preserve that glory bright and free
Let Almedore in peace, and battle gory,
Be still a nobler name for victory!

D.G.C. TO J.A.

Come, the wind may never again
Blow as now it blows for us
And the stars may never again, shine as now they shine;
Long before October returns
Seas of blood will have parted us
And you must crush the love in your heart
And I, the love in mine!

For face to face will our kindred stand
And as they are so we shall be
Forgetting how the same sweet earth has borne and
    nourished all –
One must fight for the people's power
And one for the rights of royalty
And each be ready to give his life to work the other's
    fall –

The chance of war we cannot shun
Nor would we shrink from our fathers' cause
Nor dread Death more because the hand that gives it
    may be dear
We must bear to see Ambition rule
Over Love, with his iron laws;
Must yield our blood for a stranger's sake and refuse
    ourselves a tear!

So, the wind may never again
Blow as now it blows for us
And the stars may never again shine as now they shine
Next October, the cannon's roar
From hostile ranks may be urging us —
Me to strike for your life's blood and you to strike for
     mine —

A.G.A. TO A.S.

O wander not so far away!
O love, forgive this selfish tear.
It may be sad for thee to stay
But how can I live lonely here?

The still May morn is warm and bright
Young flowers look fresh and grass is green
And in the haze of glorious light
Our long low hills are scarcely seen —

The woods — even now their small leaves hide
The blackbird and the stockdove well
And high in heaven so blue and wide
A thousand strains of music swell —

He looks on all with eyes that speak
So deep, so drear a woe to me!
There is a faint red on his cheek
Not like the bloom I used to see.

Can Death – yes, Death, he is thine own!
The grave must close those limbs around
And hush, for ever hush the tone
I loved above all earthly sound.

Well, pass away with the other flowers
Too dark for them, too dark for thee
Are the hours to come, the joyless hours
That Time is treasuring up for me.

If thou hast sinned in this world of care
'Twas but the dust of thy drear abode –
Thy soul was pure when it entered here
And pure it will go again to God –

GLENEDEN'S DREAM

Tell me, watcher, is it winter?
Say how long my sleep has been?
Have the woods I left so lovely,
Lost their robes of tender green?

Is the morning slow in coming?
Is the nighttime loath to go?
Tell me, are the dreary mountains
Drearier still with drifted snow?

'Captive, since thou sawest the forest
All its leaves have died away
And another March has woven
Garlands for another May –

'Ice has barred the Arctic water,
Soft south winds have set it free
And once more to deep green valley
Golden flowers might welcome thee' –

Watcher, in this lonely prison,
Shut from joy and kindly air
Heaven, descending in a vision
Taught my soul to do and bear –

It was night, a night of winter;
I lay on the dungeon floor,
And all other sounds were silent –
All, except the river's roar –

Over Death, and Desolation,
Fireless hearths, and lifeless homes
Over orphans' heart-sick sorrows,
Over fathers' bloody tombs;

Over friends that my arms never
Might embrace, in love again –
Memory pondered until madness
Struck its poignard in my brain –

Deepest slumber followed raving
Yet, methought, I brooded still
Still I saw my country bleeding
Dying for a Tyrant's will –

Not because *my* bliss was blasted
Burned within, the avenging flame –
Not because my scattered kindred
Died in woe, or lived in shame

God doth know, I would have given
Every bosom dear to me
Could that sacrifice have purchased
Tortured Gondal's liberty!

But, that at Ambition's bidding
All her cherished hopes should wane;
That her noblest sons should muster,
Strive, and fight and fall in vain –

Hut and castle, hall and cottage,
Roofless, crumbling to the ground –
Mighty Heaven, a glad Avenger
Thy eternal justice found!

Yes, the arm that once would shudder
Even to pierce a wounded deer,
I beheld it, unrelenting,
Choke in blood its sovereign's prayer –

Glorious dream! I saw the city
Blazing in imperial shine;
And among adoring thousands
Stood a man of form divine –

None need point the princely victim
Now he smiles with royal pride!
Now his glance is bright as lightning:
Now – the knife is in his side!

Ha, I saw how Death could darken –
Darken that triumphant eye!
His red heart's blood drenched my dagger;
My ear drank his dying sigh!

Shadows come! What means this midnight?
O my God, I know it all!
Know the fever-dream is over;
Unavenged the Avengers fall!

SONG

King Julius left the south country
His banners all bravely flying
His followers went out with Jubilee
But they shall return with sighing

Loud arose the triumphal hymn
The drums were loudly rolling
Yet you might have heard in distance dim
How a passing bell was tolling

The sword so bright from battles won
With unseen rust is fretting
The evening comes before the noon
The scarce risen sun is setting

While princes hang upon his breath
And nations round are fearing
Close by his side a daggered Death
With sheathless point stands sneering

That death he took a certain aim
For Death is stony-hearted
And in the zenith of his fame
Both power and life departed –

LINES BY CLAUDIA

I did not sleep 'twas noon of day
I saw the burning sunshine fall
The long grass bending where I lay
The blue sky brooding over all

I heard the mellow hum of bees
And singing birds and sighing trees
And far away in woody dell
The Music of the Sabbath bell

I did not dream remembrance still
Clasped round my heart its fetters chill
But I am sure the soul is free
To leave its clay a little while
Or how in exile misery
Could I have seen my country smile

In English fields my limbs were laid
With English turf beneath my head
My spirit wandered o'er that shore
Where nought but it may wander more

Yet if the soul can thus return
I need not and I will not mourn
And vainly did you drive me far
With leagues of ocean stretched between
My mortal flesh you might debar
But not the eternal fire within

My Monarch died to rule forever
A heart that can forget him never
And dear to me aye doubly dear
Thought shut within the silent tomb
His name shall be for whom I bear
This long sustained and hopeless doom

And brighter in the hour of woe
Than in the blaze of victory's pride
That glory shedding star shall glow
For which we fought and bled and died

FROM OUR EVENING
FIRESIDE NOW

From our evening fireside now,
Merry laugh and cheerful tone,
Smiling eye and cloudless brow,
Mirth and music all are flown:

Yet the grass before the door
Grows as green in April rain;
And as blithely as of yore
Larks have poured their day-long strain.

Is it fear, or is it sorrow
Checks the stagnant stream of joy?
Do we tremble that tomorrow
May our present peace destroy?

For past misery are we weeping?
What is past can hurt no more;
And the gracious heavens are keeping
Aid for that which lies before –

One is absent, and for one
Cheerless, chill is our hearthstone –
One is absent, and for him
Cheeks are pale and eyes are dim –

Arthur, brother, Gondal's shore
Rested from the battle's roar –
Arthur, brother, we returned
Back to Desmond lost and mourned:

Thou didst purchase by thy fall
Home for us and peace for all;
Yet, how darkly dawned that day –
Dreadful was the price to pay!

Just as once, through sun and mist
I have climbed the mountain's breast
Still my gun with certain aim
Brought to earth the fluttering game:

But the very dogs repined,
Though I called with whistle shrill
Listlessly they lagged behind,
Looking backward o'er the hill –

Sorrow was not vocal there:
Mute their pain and my despair
But the joy of life was flown
He was gone, and we were lone –

So it is by morn and eve —
So it is in field and hall —
For the absent one we grieve,
One being absent saddens All —

HOW LONG WILL YOU REMAIN?

How long will you remain? The midnight hour
Has tolled the last note from the minster tower
Come come the fire is dead the lamp burns low
Your eyelids droop a weight is on your brow
Your cold hands hardly hold the useless pen
Come morn will give recovered strength again

No let me linger leave me let me be
A little longer in this reverie
I'm happy now and would you tear away
My blissful dream that never comes with day
A vision dear though false for well my mind
Knows what a bitter waking waits behind

Can there be pleasure in this shadowy room
With windows yawning on intenser gloom
And such a dreary wind so bleakly sweeping
Round walls where only you are vigil keeping
Besides your face has not a sign of joy
And more than tearful sorrow fills your eye
Look on those woods look on that heaven lorn
And think how changed they'll be tomorrow morn

The dome of heaven expanding bright and blue
The leaves the green grass sprinkled thick with dew
And wet mists rising on the river's breast
And wild birds bursting from their songless nest
And your own children's merry voices chasing
The fancies grief not pleasure has been tracing

Aye speak of these – but can you tell me why
Day breathes such beauty over earth and sky
And waking sounds revive restore again
Dull hearts that all night long have throbbed in pain

Is it not that the sunshine and the wind
Lure from its self the mourner's woe worn mind
And all the joyous music breathing by
And all the splendour of that cloudless sky

Regive him shadowy gleams of infancy
And draw his tired gaze from futurity

SONG BY JULIUS
BRENZAIDA

Geraldine, the moon is shining
With so soft, so bright a ray,
Seems it not that eve, declining
Ushered in a fairer day?

While the wind is whispering only,
Far – across the water borne
Let us, in this silence lonely
Sit beneath the ancient thorn –

Wild the road, and rough and dreary;
Barren all the moorland round;
Rude the couch that rests us weary;
Mossy stone and heathy ground –

But when winter storms were meeting
In the moonless midnight dome
Did we heed the tempest's beating
Howling round our spirits' home?

No, that tree, with branches riven
Whitening in the whirl of snow,
As it tossed against the heaven,
Sheltered happy hearts below –

And at Autumn's mild returning
Shall our feet forget the way?
And in Cynthia's silver morning
Geraldine will thou de lay?

SONG BY J. BRENZAIDA
TO G.S.

I knew not 'twas so dire a crime
To say the word, Adieu:
But this shall be the only time
My slighted heart shall sue.

The wild moorside, the winter morn,
The gnarled and ancient tree –
If in your breast they waken scorn
Shall wake the same in me.

I can forget black eyes and brows
And lips of rosy charm
If you forget the sacred vows
Those faithless lips could form –

If hard commands can tame your love,
Or prison walls can hold
I would not wish to grieve above
A thing so false and cold –

And there are bosoms bound to mine
With links both tried and strong;
And there are eyes whose lightning shine
Has warmed and blessed me long:

Those eyes shall make my only day,
Shall set my spirit free
And chase the foolish thoughts away
That shroud your memory!

NONE OF MY KINDRED NOW CAN TELL

None of my kindred now can tell
The features once beloved so well
Those dark brown locks that used to deck
A snowy brow in ringlets small
Now wildly shade my sunburnt neck
And streaming down my shoulders fall

The pure bright red of noble birth
Has deepened to a gipsy glow
And care has quenched the smile of mirth
And tuned my heart to welcome woe

Yet you must know in infancy
Full many an eye watched over me
Sweet voices to my slumber sung
My downy couch with silk was hung

And music soothed me when I cried
And when I laughed they all replied
And 'rosy Blanche' how oft was heard
In hall and bower that well-known word

Through gathering summers still caress'd
In kingly courts a favourite guest
A Monarch's hand would pour for me
The richest gifts of royalty

But clouds will come too soon they came
For not through age and not through crime
Is Blanche a now forgotten name
True heart and brow unmarked by time
These treasured blessings still are mine

A.G.A. TO A.S.

This summer wind, with thee and me
Roams in the dawn of day;
But thou must be where it shall be,
Ere Evening – far away.

The farewell's echo from thy soul
Should not depart before
Hills rise and distant rivers roll
Between us evermore –

I know that I have done thee wrong –
Have wronged both thee and Heaven –
And I may mourn my lifetime long
Yet may not be forgiven –

Repentant tears will vainly fall
To cancel deeds untrue;
But for no grief can I recall
The dreary word – Adieu –

Yet thou a future peace shalt win
Because thy soul is clear;
And I who had the heart to sin
Will find a heart to bear —

Till far beyond earth's frenzied strife
That makes destruction joy
Thy perished faith shall spring to life
And my remorse shall die

E.W. TO A.G.A.

How few, of all the hearts that loved,
Are grieving for thee now!
And why should mine, tonight, be moved
With such a sense of woe?

Too often, thus, when left alone
Where none my thoughts can see,
Comes back a word, a passing tone
From thy strange history.

Sometimes I seem to see thee rise
A glorious child again –
All virtues beaming from thine eyes
That ever honoured men –

Courage and Truth, a generous breast
Where Love and Gladness lay;
A being whose very Memory blest
And made the mourner gay –

O, fairly spread thy early sail
And fresh and pure and free
Was the first impulse of the gale
That urged life's wave for thee!

Why did the pilot, too confiding
Dream o'er that Ocean's foam?
And trust in Pleasure's careless guiding
To bring his vessel home?

For, well, he knew what dangers frowned,
What mists would gather dim,
What rocks and shelves and sands lay round
Between his port and him —

The very brightness of the sun,
The splendour of the main,
The wind that bore him wildly on
Should not have warned in vain

An anxious gazer from the shore,
I marked the whitening wave
And wept above thy fate the more
Because I could not save —

It recks not now, when all is over,
But, yet my heart will be
A mourner still, though friend and lover
Have both forgotten thee!

A THOUSAND SOUNDS OF HAPPINESS

A thousand sounds of happiness
And only one of real distress;
One hardly uttered groan –
But that has hushed all vocal joy,
Eclipsed the glory of the sky
And made me think that misery
Rules in our world alone!

About his face the sunshine glows
And in his hair the south wind blows
And violet and wild wood-rose
Are sweetly breathing near

Nothing without suggests dismay
If he could force his mind away
From tracking farther day by day
The desert of Despair –

Too truly agonized to weep
His eyes are motionless as sleep,
His frequent sighs long-drawn and deep
Are anguish to my ear
And I would soothe but can I call
The cold corpse from its funeral pall
And cause a gleam of hope to fall
With my consoling tear?

O Death, so many spirits driven
Through this false world, their all had given
To win the everlasting haven
To sufferers so divine –

Why didst thou smite the loved the blest
The ardent and the happy breast
That full of hope desired not rest
And shrank appalled from thine?

At least, since thou wilt not restore
In mercy launch one arrow more
Life's conscious Death it wearies sore
It tortures worse than thee –
Enough of storms have bowed his head,
Grant him at last a quiet bed
Beside his early stricken Dead
Even where he yearns to be!

WHY ASK TO KNOW THE DATE –
THE CLIME?

Why ask to know the date – the clime?
More than mere words they cannot be:
Men knelt to God and worshipped crime,
And crushed the helpless even as we –

But, they had learnt, from length of strife –
Of civil war and anarchy
To laugh at death and look on life
With somewhat lighter sympathy.

It was the autumn of the year,
The time to labouring peasants, dear:
Week after week, from noon to noon,
September shone as bright as June –
Still, never hand a sickle held;
The crops were garnered in the field –
Trod out and ground by horses' feet
While every ear was milky sweet;
And kneaded on the threshing-floor
With mire of tears and human gore.
Some said they thought that heaven's pure rain
Would hardly bless those fields again:
Not so – the all-benignant skies
Rebuked that fear of famished eyes –

July passed on with showers and dew,
And August glowed in showerless blue;
No harvest time could be more fair
Had harvest fruits but ripened there.

And I confess that hate of rest,
And thirst for things abandoned now,
Had weaned me from my country's breast
And brought me to that land of woe.

Enthusiast – in a name delighting,
My alien sword I drew to free
One race, beneath two standards fighting,
For Loyalty, and Liberty –

When kindred strive, God help the weak!
A brother's ruth 'tis vain to seek:
At first, it hurt my chivalry
To join them in their cruelty;
But I grew hard – I learnt to wear
An iron front to terror's prayer;
I learnt to turn my ears away
From torture's groans, as well as they.
By force I learnt – what power had I
To say the conquered should not die?
What heart, one trembling foe to save
When hundreds daily filled the grave?

Yet, there *were* faces that could move
A moment's flash of human love;
And there were fates that made me feel
I was not to the centre, steel –

I've often witnessed wise men fear
To meet distress which they foresaw;
And seeming cowards nobly bear
A doom that thrilled the brave with awe;

Strange proofs I've seen, how hearts could hide
Their secret with a life-long pride,
And then reveal it as they died –
Strange courage, and strange weakness too,
In that last hour when most are true,
And timid natures strangely nerved
To deeds from which the desperate swerved.
These I may tell, but leave them now.
Go with me where my thoughts would go;
Now all today and all last night
I've had one scene before my sight –

Wood-shadowed dales; a harvest moon
Unclouded in its glorious noon;
A solemn landscape, wide and still;
A red fire on a distant hill –
A line of fires, and deep below,
Another dusker, drearier glow –

Charred beams, and lime, and blackened stones
Self-piled in cairns o'er burning bones,
And lurid flames that licked the wood
Then quenched their glare in pools of blood –
But yestereve – No! never care;
Let street and suburb smoulder there –
Smoke-hidden, in the winding glen,
They lay too far to vex my ken.
Four score shot down – all veterans strong –
One prisoner spared, their leader young –
And he within his house was laid,
Wounded, and weak and nearly dead.
We gave him life against his will;
For he entreated us to kill –
But statue-like we saw his tears –
And harshly fell our captain's sneers!

'Now, heaven forbid!' with scorn he said –
'That noble gore our hands should shed
Like common blood – retain thy breath
Or scheme, if thou canst purchase death –
When men are poor we sometimes hear
And pitying grant that dastard prayer;
When men are rich, we make them buy
The pleasant privilege, to die –
O, we have castles reared for kings
Embattled towers and buttressed wings

Thrice three feet thick, and guarded well
With chain, and bolt, and sentinel!
We build our despots' dwellings sure;
Knowing they love to live secure –
And our respect for royalty
Extends to thy estate and thee!'

The suppliant groaned; his moistened eye
Swam wild and dim with agony –
The gentle blood could ill sustain
Degrading taunts, unhonoured pain.
Bold had he shown himself to lead;
Eager to smite and proud to bleed –
A man amid the battle's storm;
An infant in the after calm.

Beyond the town his mansion stood
Girt round with pasture-land and wood;
And there our wounded soldiers lying
Enjoyed the ease of wealth in dying:

For him, no mortal more than he
Had softened life with luxury;
And truly did our priest declare
'Of good things he had had his share.'

We lodged him in an empty place,
The full moon beaming on his face
Through shivered glass, and ruins, made
Where shell and ball the fiercest played.
I watched his ghastly couch beside
Regardless if he lived or died –
Nay, muttering curses on the breast
Whose ceaseless moans denied me rest:

'Twas hard, I know, 'twas harsh to say,
'Hell snatch thy worthless soul away!'
But then 'twas hard my life to keep
Through this long night, estranged from sleep.
Captive and keeper, both outworn,
Each in his misery yearned for morn;
Even though returning morn should bring
Intenser toil and suffering.

Slow, slow it came! Our dreary room
Grew drearier with departing gloom;
Yet as the west wind warmly blew
I felt my pulses bound anew,
And turned to him – nor breeze, nor ray
Revived that mould of shattered clay,
Scarce conscious of his pain he lay –
Scarce conscious that my hands removed
The glittering toys his lightness loved –

The jewelled rings, and locket fair
Where rival curls of silken hair,
Sable and brown revealed to me
A tale of doubtful constancy.

'Forsake the world without regret,'
I murmured in contemptuous tone;
'The world, poor wretch, will soon forget
Thy noble name when thou art gone!
Happy, if years of slothful shame
Could perish like a noble name –
If God did no account require
And being with breathing might expire!'
And words of such contempt I said,
Cold insults o'er a dying bed,
Which as they darken memory now
Disturb my pulse and flush my brow;
I know that Justice holds in store,
Reprisals for those days of gore –
Not for the blood, but for the sin
Of stifling mercy's voice within.
The blood spilt gives no pang at all;
It is my conscience haunting me,
Telling how oft my lips shed gall
On many a thing too weak to be,
Even in thought, my enemy –
And whispering ever, when I pray,

'God will repay – God will repay!'
He does repay and soon and well
The deeds that turn his earth to hell
The wrongs that aim a venomed dart
Through nature at the Eternal Heart –
Surely my cruel tongue was cursed
I know my prisoner heard me speak
A transient gleam of feeling burst
And wandered o'er his haggard cheek
And from his quivering lids there stole
A look to melt a demon's soul
A silent prayer more powerful far
Than any breathed petitions are
Pleading in mortal agony
To mercy's Source but not to me –
Now I recall that glance and groan
And wring my hands in vain distress
Then I was adamantine stone
Nor felt one touch of tenderness –
My plunder ta'en I left him there
Without one breath of morning air
To struggle with his last despair
Regardless of the wildered cry
Which wailed for death yet wailed to die
I left him there unwatched alone
And eager sought the court below
Where o'er a trough of chiselled stone

An ice cold well did gurgling flow
The water in its basin shed
A stranger tinge of fiery red.
I drank and scarcely marked the hue
My food was dyed with crimson too
As I went out a ragged child
With wasted cheek and ringlets wild
A shape of fear and misery
Raised up her helpless hands to me
And begged her father's face to see
I spurned the piteous wretch away
Thy father's face is lifeless clay
As thine mayst be ere fall of day
Unless the truth be quickly told
Where thou hast hid thy father's gold
Yet in the intervals of pain
He heard my taunts and moaned again
And mocking moans did I reply
And asked him why he would not die
In noble agony – uncomplaining.
Was it not foul disgrace and shame
To thus disgrace his ancient name?
Just then a comrade came hurrying in
Alas, he cried, sin genders sin
For every soldier slain they've sworn
To hang up five come morn.
They've ta'en of stranglers sixty-three

Full thirty from one company
And all my father's family
And comrade thou hadst only one
They've ta'en thy all thy little son
Down at my captive's feet I fell
I had no option in despair
As thou wouldst save thy soul from hell
My heart's own darling bid them spare
Or human hate and hate divine
Blight every orphan flower of thine
He raised his head – from death beguiled
He wakened up he almost smiled
Twice in my arms twice on my knee
You stabbed my child and laughed at me
And so, with choking voice he said
I trust I hope in God she's dead
Yet not to thee not even to thee
Would I return such misery
Such is that fearful grief I know
I will not cause thee equal woe
Write that they harm no infant there
Write that it is my latest prayer
I wrote – he signed and thus did save
My treasure from the gory grave
And O my soul longed wildly then
To give his saviour life again.
But heedless of my gratitude

The silent corpse before me lay
And still methinks in gloomy mood
I see it fresh as yesterday
The sad face raised imploringly
To mercy's God and not to me –
The last look of that agony
I could not rescue him his child
I found alive and tended well
But she was full of anguish wild
And hated me like we hate hell
And weary with her savage woe
One moonless night I let her go

SONG TO A.A.

This shall be thy lullaby
Rocking on the stormy sea
Though it roar in thunder wild
Sleep stilly sleep my dark haired child

When our shuddering boat was crossing
Elderno lake so rudely tossing
Then 'twas first my nursling smiled
Sleep softly sleep my fair-browed child

Waves above thy cradle break
Foamy tears are on thy cheek
Yet the Ocean's self grows mild
When it bears my slumbering child

WHY DO I HATE THAT
LONE GREEN DELL?

Why do I hate that lone green dell?
Buried in moors and mountains wild
That is a spot I had loved too well
Had I but seen it when a child

There are bones whitening there in the summer's heat
But it is not for that and none can tell
None but one can the secret repeat
Why I hate that lone green dell

Noble foe I pardon thee
All thy cold and scornful pride
For thou wast a priceless friend to me
When my sad heart had none beside

And leaning on thy generous arm
A breath of old times over me came
The earth shone round with a long lost charm
Alas I forgot I was not the same

Before a day – an hour passed by
My spirit knew itself once more
I saw the gilded vapours fly
And leave me as I was before

E.G. TO M.R.

Thy Guardians are asleep
So I've come to bid thee rise;
Thou hast a holy vow to keep
Ere yon crescent quit the skies:

Though clouds careering wide
Will hardly let her gleam
She's bright enough to be our guide
Across the mountain-stream –

O waken, Dearest, wake!
What means this long delay?
Say, wilt thou not for honour's sake
Chase idle fears away?

Think not of future grief
Entailed on present joy:
An age of woe were only brief
Its memory to destroy –

And neither Hell nor Heaven
Though both conspire at last
Can take the bliss that has been given –
Can rob us of the past –

Then, waken, Mary, wake
How canst thou linger now?
For true love's and Gleneden's sake
Arise and keep thy vow!

TO A.G.A.

'Thou standest in the greenwood now
The place, the hour, the same –
And here the fresh leaves gleam and glow
And there, down in the lake below
The tiny ripples flame –

'The breeze sings like a summer breeze
Should sing in summer skies
And tower-like rocks and tent-like trees
In mingled glory rise.

'But where is he today, today?'
'O question not with me' –
'I will not, Lady, only say
Where may thy lover be?

'Is he upon some distant shore?
Or is he on the sea?
Or is the heart thou dost adore,
A faithless heart to thee?'

'The heart I love, whate'er betide,
Is faithful as the grave
And neither foreign lands divide
Nor yet the rolling wave.'

'Then why should sorrow cloud that brow,
And tears those eyes bedim?
Reply this once, is it that thou
Hast faithless been to him?'

'I gazed upon the cloudless moon
And loved her all the night
Till morning came and ardent noon
Then I forgot her light –

'No – not forgot, eternally
Remains its memory dear;
But could the day seem dark to me
Because the night was fair?'

'I well may mourn that only one
Can light my future sky
Even though by such a radiant sun
My moon of life must die' –

ON THE FALL OF ZALONA

All blue and bright, in glorious light
The morn comes marching on
And now Zalona's steeples white
Glow golden in the sun –

This day might be a festal day;
The streets are crowded all,
And emerald flags stream broad and gay
From turret, tower and wall;

And hark! how music, evermore
Is sounding in the sky:
The deep bells boom – the cannon roar,
The trumpets sound on high –

The deep bells boom, the deep bells clash
Upon the reeling air:
The cannon, with unceasing crash
Make answer far and near –

What do those brazen tongues proclaim?
What joyous fête begun –
What offering to our country's fame –
What noble victory won?

Go, ask that solitary sire
Laid in his house alone;
His silent hearth without a fire –
His sons and daughters gone –

Go, ask those children, in the street
Beside their mother's door;
Waiting to hear the lingering feet
That they shall hear no more.

Ask those pale soldiers round the gates
With famine-kindled eye –
They'll say, 'Zalona celebrates
The day that she must die!'

The charger, by his manger tied
Has rested many a day;
Yet ere the spur have touched his side,
Behold, he sinks away!

And hungry dogs, with wolf-like cry
Unburied corpses tear,
While their gaunt masters gaze and sigh
And scarce the feast forbear –

Now, look down from Zalona's wall —
There war the unwearied foe:
If ranks before our cannon fall,
New ranks, forever, grow —

And many a week, unbroken thus,
Their troops, our ramparts hem;
And for each man that fights for us
A hundred fight for them!

Courage and Right and spotless Truth
Were pitched 'gainst traitor sull vim
We offered all our age, our youth —
Our brave men in their prime —

And all have failed! the fervent prayers,
The trust in heavenly aid,
Valour and faith and sealed tears
That would not mourn the dead —

Lips, that did breathe no murmuring word;
Hearts, that did ne'er complain
Though vengeance held a sheathed sword
And martyrs bled in vain —

Alas, alas, the Myrtle bowers
By blighting blasts destroyed!
Alas, the Lily's withered flowers
That leave the garden void!

Unfolds o'er tower, and waves o'er height,
A sheet of crimson sheen –
Is it the setting sun's red light
That stains our standard green?

Heaven help us in this awful hour!
For now might Faith decay –
Now might we doubt God's guardian power
And curse, instead of pray –

He will not even let us die –
Not let us die at home;
The foe must see our soldiers fly
As they had feared the Tomb:

Because, we *dare* not stay to gain
Those longed for, glorious graves –
We dare not shrink from slavery's chain
To leave our children slaves!

But when this scene of awful woe
Has neared its final close
As God forsook our armies, so
May He forsake our foes!

FROM A DUNGEON WALL IN THE SOUTHERN COLLEGE

'Listen! when your hair like mine
Takes a tint of silver grey,
When your eyes, with dimmer shine,
Watch life's bubbles float away,

'When you, young man, have borne like me
The weary weight of sixty-three
Then shall penance sore be paid
For these hours so wildly squandered
And the words that now fall dead
On your ears be deeply pondered
Pondered and approved at last
But their virtue will be past!

'Glorious is the prize of Duty
Though she be a serious power
Treacherous all the lures of Beauty
Thorny bud and poisonous flower!

'Mirth is but a mad beguiling
Of the golden gifted Time –
Love – a demon meteor wiling
Heedless feet to gulfs of crime.

'Those who follow earthly pleasure
Heavenly Knowledge will not lead
Wisdom hides from them her treasure,
Virtue bids them evil speed!

'Vainly may their hearts, repenting,
Seek for aid in future years –
Wisdom scorned knows no relenting –
Virtue is not won by tears

'Fain would we your steps reclaim
Waken fear and holy shame
And to this end, our council well
And kindly doomed you to a cell
Whose darkness, may perchance, disclose
A beacon-guide from sterner woes' –

So spake my judge – then seized his lamp
And left me in the dungeon damp,
A vault-like place whose stagnant air
Suggests and nourishes despair!

Rosina, this had never been
Except for you, my despot queen!
Except for you the billowy sea
Would now be tossing under me
The wind's wild voice my bosom thrill
And my glad heart bound wilder still

Flying before the rapid gale
Those wondrous southern isles to hail
Which wait for my companions free
But thank your passion – not for me!

You know too well – and so do I
Your haughty beauty's sovereignty
Yet have I read those falcon eyes –
Have dived into their mysteries –
Have studied long their glance and feel
It is not love those eyes reveal –

They Flash – they burn with lightning shine
But not with such fond fire as mine;
The tender star fades faint and wan
Before Ambition's scorching sun –
So deem I now – and Time will prove
If I have wronged Rosina's love –

M.A. WRITTEN ON THE
DUNGEON WALL – N.C.

I know that tonight, the wind is sighing,
The soft August wind, over forest and moor
While I in a grave-like chill am lying
On the damp black flags of my dungeon-floor –

I know that the Harvest Moon is shining;
She neither will wax nor wane for me,
Yet I weary, weary, with vain repining,
One gleam of her heaven-bright face to hail

For this night and darkness is wasting the gladness
Wasting the gladness of life away;
It gathers up thoughts akin to madness
That never would cloud the world of day

I chide with my soul – I bid it cherish
The feelings it lived on when I was free,
But, shrinking it murmurs, 'Let Memory perish
Forget for thy Friends have forgotten thee!'

Alas, I did think that they were weeping
Such tears as I weep – it is not so!
Their careless young eyes are closed in sleeping;
Their brows are unshadowed, undimmed by woe –

Might I go to their beds, I'd rouse that slumber,
My spirit should startle their rest, and tell
How hour after hour, I wakefully number
Deep buried from light in my lonely cell!

Yet let them dream on, though dreary dreaming
Would haunt my pillow if *they* were here
And *I* were laid warmly under the gleaming
Of that guardian moon and her comrade star –

Better that I my own fate mourning
Should pine alone in the prison-gloom
Than waken free on the summer morning
And feel they were suffering this awful doom

RODRIC LESLEY. 1830

Lie down and rest, the fight is done
Thy comrades to the camp retire;
Gaze not so earnestly upon
The far gleam of the beacon fire.

Listen not to the wind-borne sounds
Of music and of soldiers' cheer,
Thou canst not go – unnumbered wounds
Exhaust thy life and hold thee here –

Had that hand power to raise the sword
Which since this morn laid hundreds low
Had that tongue strength to speak the word
That urged thy followers on the foe

Were that warm blood within thy veins
Which now upon the earth is flowing
Splashing its sod with crimson stains
Reddening the pale heath round thee growing

Then Rodric, thou might'st still be turning
With eager eye and anxious breast
To where those signal-lights are burning –
To where thy monarch's legions rest –

But never more – Look up and see
The twilight fading from the skies
That last dim beam that sets for thee,
Rodric, for thee shall never rise!

M.G. FOR THE U.S.

'Twas yesterday at early dawn
I watched the falling snow;
A drearier scene on winter morn
Was never stretched below.

I could not see the mountains round
But I knew by the wild wind's roar
How every drift, in their glens profound
Was deepening ever more –

And then I thought of Ula's bowers
Beyond the southern sea
Her tropic prairies bright with flowers
And rivers wandering free –

I thought of many a happy day
Spent in her Eden isle
With my dear comrades, young and gay
All scattered now so far away
But not forgot the while!

Who that has breathed that heavenly air
To northern climes would come
To Gondal's mists and moorlands drear
And sleet and frozen gloom?

Spring brings the swallow and the lark
But what will winter bring?
Its twilight noons and evenings dark
To match the gifts of spring?

No, Look with me o'er that sullen main
If thy spirit's eye can see
There are brave ships floating back again
That no calm southern port could chain
From Gondal's stormy sea.

O how the hearts of the voyagers beat
To feel the frost-wind blow!
What flower in Ula's gardens sweet
Is worth one flake of snow?

The blast which almost rends their sail
Is welcome as a friend;
It brings them home, that thundering gale
Home to their journey's end:

Home to our souls whose wearying sighs
Lament their absence drear
And feel how bright even winter skies
Would shine if they were here!

AT CASTLE WOOD

The day is done – the winter sun
Is setting in its sullen sky
And drear the course that has been run
And dim the hearts that slowly die

No star will light my coming night
No morn of hope for me will shine
I mourn not heaven would blast my sight
And I never longed for ways divine

Through Life's hard Task I did not ask
Celestial nor celestial cheer
I saw my fate without its mask
And met it too without a tear

The grief that pressed this living breast
Was heavier far than earth can be
And who would dread eternal rest
When labour's hire was agony

Dark falls the fear of this despair
On spirits born for happiness
But I was bred the mate of care
The foster child of sore distress

No sighs for me, no sympathy,
No wish to keep my soul below
The heart is dead since infancy
Unwept for let the body go

A.S. TO G.S.

I do not weep, I would not weep;
Our Mother needs no tears:
Dry thine eyes too, 'tis vain to keep
This causeless grief for years

What though her brow be changed and cold,
Her sweet eyes closed for ever?
What though the stone – the darksome mould
Our mortal bodies sever?

What though her hand caress ne'er again
Those silken locks of thine –
Nor through long hours of future pain
Her kind face o'er thee shine?

Remember still she is not dead
She sees us Gerald now
Laid where her angel spirit fled
'Mid heath and frozen snow

And from that world of heavenly light
Will she not always bend
To guide us in our lifetime's night
And guard us to the end?

Thou know'st she will, and well may'st mourn
That we are left below
But not that she can ne'er return
To share our earthly woe –

O MOTHER I AM NOT REGRETTING

O mother I am not regretting
To leave this wretched world below
If there be nothing but forgetting
In that dark land to which I go

Yet though 'tis wretched now to languish
Deceived and tired and hopeless here
No heart can quite repress the anguish
Of leaving things that once were dear

Twice twelve short years and all is over
And day and night to rise no more
And never more to be a rover
Along the fields the woods the shore

And never more at early dawning
To watch the stars of midnight wane
To breathe the breath of summer morning
And see its sunshine ne'er again

I hear the Abbey bells are ringing
Methinks their chime sound faint and drear
Or else the wind is adverse winging
And wafts its music from my ear

The wind the winter night is speaking
Of thoughts and things that should not stay
Mother come near my heart is breaking
I cannot bear to go away

And I *must* go whence no returning
To soothe your grief or calm your care
Nay do not weep that bitter mourning
Tortures my soul with wild despair

No tell me that when I am lying
In the old church beneath the stone
You'll dry your tears and check your sighing
And soon forget the spirit gone

You've asked me long to tell what sorrow
Has blanched my cheek and quenched my eye
And we shall sever ere tomorrow
So I'll confess before I die

Ten years ago in last September
Fernando left his home and you
And still I think you must remember
The anguish of that last adieu

And well you know how wildly pining
I longed to see his face again
Through all the Autumn's drear declining
Its stormy nights and days of rain

Down on the skirts of Areon's forest
There lies a lone and lovely glade
And there the hearts together nourished
Their first their fatal parting made

The afternoon in softened glory
So Bathed each green swell and waving tree
Beyond the broad park spread before me
Stretched far away the boundless sea

And there I stood when he had left me
With ashy cheek but tearless eye
Watching the ship whose sail bereft me
Of life and hope and peace and joy

It past that night I sought a pillow
Of sleepless woe and grieving lone
My soul still hovered o'er the billow
And mourned a love for ever flown

Yet smiling bright in recollection
One blissful hour returns to me
One letter told of firm affection
Of safe deliverance from the sea

But not another fearing hoping
Spring winter harvest glided o'er
And time at length brought power for coping
With thoughts I could not once endure

And I would seek in summer's evening
The place that saw our last farewell
And there a chain of visions weaving
I'd linger till the curfew bell

H.A. AND A.S.

In the same place, when Nature wore
The same celestial glow;
I'm sure I've seen those forms before
But many springs ago;

And only *he* had locks of light
And *she* had raven hair,
While now, his curls are dark as night
And hers, as morning fair.

Besides, I've dreamt of things whose traces
Will never more depart
In agony that fast effaces
The verdure of the heart —

I dreamt one sunny day like this
In this peerless month of May
I saw her give the unanswered kiss
As his spirit passed away:

Those young eyes that so sweetly shine
Then looked their last adieu
And pale Death changed that cheek divine
To his unchanging hue

And earth was cast above the breast
That beats so warm and free
Where her soft ringlets lightly rest
And move responsively

Then she, upon the covered grave –
The grass grown grave, did lie –
A tomb not girt by Gondal's wave
Nor arched by Gondal's sky.

The sod was sparkling bright with dew
But brighter still with tears
That welled from mortal grief, I knew
Which never heals with years -

And if he came not for her woe
He would not now return;
He would not leave his sleep below
When she had ceased to mourn –

O Innocence, that cannot live
With heart-wrung anguish long
Dear childhood's Innocence, forgive,
For I have done thee wrong!

The bright rosebuds, those hawthorns shroud
Within their perfumed bower
Have never closed beneath a cloud
Nor bent before a shower –

Had darkness once obscured their sun
Or kind dew turned to rain
No storm-cleared sky that ever shone
Could win such bliss again –

NOW TRUST A HEART
THAT TRUSTS IN YOU

Now trust a heart that trusts in you
And firmly say the word Adieu
Be sure wherever I may roam
My heart is with your heart at home

Unless there be no truth on earth
And vows meant true are nothing worth
And mortal man have no control
Over his own unhappy soul

Unless I change in every thought
And memory will restore me nought
And all I have of virtue die
Beneath far Gondal's Foreign sky

The mountain peasant loves the heath
Better than richest plains beneath
He would not give one moorland wild
For all the fields that ever smiled

And whiter brows than yours may be
And rosier cheeks my eyes may see
And lightning looks from orbs divine
About my pathway burn and shine

But that pure light changeless and strong
Cherished and watched and nursed so long
That love that first its glory gave
Shall be my pole star to the grave

STRONG I STAND

Strong I stand though I have borne
Anger hate and bitter scorn
Strong I stand and laugh to see
How mankind have fought with me

Shade of mast'ry I contemn
All the puny ways of men
Free my heart my spirit free
Beckon and I'll follow thee

False and foolish mortal know
If you scorn the world's disdain
Your mean soul is far below
Other worms however vain

Thing of Dust – with boundless pride
Dare you ask me for a guide
With the humble I will be
Haughty men are nought to me

THE ORGAN SWELLS
THE TRUMPETS SOUND

The organ swells the trumpets sound
The lamps in triumph glow
And none of all those thousands round
Regards who sleeps below

Those haughty eyes that tears should fill
Glance clearly cloudlessly
Those bounding breasts that grief should thrill
From thought of grief are free

His subjects and his soldiers there
They blessed his rising bloom
But none a single sigh can spare
To breathe above his tomb

Comrades in arms I've looked to mark
One shade of feeling swell
As your feet trod above the dark
Recesses of his cell

A SUDDEN CHASM OF GHASTLY LIGHT

A sudden chasm of ghastly light
Yawned in the city's reeling wall
And a long thundering through the night
Proclaimed our triumph – Tyrdarum's fall –

The shrieking wind sank mute and mild
The smothering snow-clouds rolled away
And cold – how cold! – wan moonlight smiled
Where those black ruins smouldering lay

'Twas over – all the Battle's madness
The bursting fires the cannons' roar
The yells, the groans the frenzied gladness
The death the danger warmed no more

In plundered churches piled with dead
The heavy charger neighed for food
The wounded soldier laid his head
'Neath roofless chambers splashed with blood

I could not sleep through that wild siege
My heart had fiercely burned and bounded
The outward tumult seemed to assuage
The inward tempest it surrounded

But . . . cannot bear
And silence whets the tang of pain
I felt the full flood of despair
Returning to my breast again

My couch lay in a ruined Hall
Whose windows looked on the minster-yard
Where chill chill whiteness covered all
Both stone and urn and withered sward

The shattered glass let in the air
And with it came a wandering moan
A sound unutterably drear
That made me shrink to be alone

One black yew-tree grew just below
I thought its boughs so sad might wail
Their ghostly fingers flecked with snow
Rattled against an old vault's rail

I listened – no 'twas life that still
Lingered in some deserted heart
O God what caused that shuddering thrill?
That anguished agonizing start?

An undefined an awful dream
A dream of what had been before
A memory whose blighting beam
Was flitting o'er me ever more

A frightful feeling frenzy born —
I hurried down the dark oak stair
I reached the door whose hinges torn
Flung streaks of moonshine here and there

I pondered not I drew the bar
An icy glory caught mine eye
From that wide heaven where every star
Glared like a dying memory

And there the great cathedral rose
Discrowned but most majestic so
It looked down in serene repose
On its own realm of buried woe

COMPANIONS, ALL DAY LONG
WE'VE STOOD

Companions, all day long we've stood
The wild winds restless blowing
All day we've watched the darkened flood
Around our vessel flowing

Sunshine has never smiled since morn
And clouds have gathered drear
And heavier hearts would feel forlorn
And weaker minds would fear

But look in my young shipmate's eyes
I lit by the evening flame
And see how little stormy skies
Our joyous blood can tame

No glance the same expression wears
No lip the same soft smile
Yet kindness warms and courage cheers
Nerves every breast the while

It is the hour of dreaming now
The red fire brightly gleams
And sweetest in a red fire's glow
The hour of dreaming seems

I may not trace the thoughts of all
But some I read as well
As I can hear the ocean's fall
And sullen surging swell

Edmund's swift soul is gone before
It threads a forest wide
Whose towers are bending to the shore
And gazing on the tide

And one is there – I know the voice
The thrilling stirring tone
That makes his bounding pulse rejoice
Yet makes not *his* alone

Mine own hand longs to clasp her hand
Mine eye to greet her eye
Win white sails, win Zedora's strand
And Ula's Eden sky –

Mary and Flora oft their gaze
Is clouded pensively
And what that earnest aspect says
Is all revealed to me

'Tis but two years or little more
Since first they dared that main
And such a night may well restore
That first time back again

The smothered sigh the lingering late
The longed for dreaded hour
The parting at the moss-grown gate
The last look on the tower

I know they think of these and then
The evening's gathering gloom
And they alone with forign men
To guard their waldli room

THERE SHINES THE MOON

There shines the moon, at noon of night –
Vision of glory – Dream of light!
Holy as heaven – undimmed and pure,
Looking down on the lonely moor –
And lonelier still beneath her ray
That drear moor stretches far away
Till it seems strange that aught can lie
Beyond its zone of silver sky –

Bright moon – dear moon! when years have past
My weary feet return at last –
And still upon Lake Elnor's breast
Thy solemn rays serenely rest
And still the Fern-leaves sighing wave
Like mourners over Elbë's grave
And Earth's the same but Oh to see
How wildly Time has altered me!
Am I the being who long ago
Sat watching by that water side
The light of life expiring slow
From his fair cheek and brow of pride?
Not oft these mountains feel the shine
Of such a day – as fading then,
Cast from its fount of gold divine
A last smile on the heathery plain

And kissed the far-off peaks of snow
That gleaming on the horizon shone
As if in summer's warmest glow
Stern winter claimed a loftier throne –
And there he lay among the bloom
His red blood dyed a deeper hue
Shuddering to feel the ghostly gloom
That coming Death around him threw –
Sickening to think one hour would sever
The sweet, sweet world and him forever
To think that twilight gathering dim
Would never pass away to him –
No – never more! That awful thought
A thoughtful dreary feelings brought,
And memory all her powers combined
And rushed upon his fainting mind.
Wide, swelling woodlands seemed to rise
Beneath soft, sunny, southern skies –
Old Elbë Hall his noble home
Towered 'mid its trees, whose foliage green
Rustled with the kind airs that come
From summer Heavens when most serene
And bursting through the leafy shade
A gush of golden sunshine played;
Bathing the walls in amber light
And sparkling in the water clear
That stretched below – reflected bright

The whole wide world of cloudless air –
And still before his spirit's eye
Such well known scenes would rise and fly
Till, maddening with despair and pain
He turned his dying face to me
And wildly cried, 'Oh once again
Might I my native country see!
But once again – one single day!
And must it – can it *never* be?
To die – and die so far away
When life has hardly smiled for me –
Augusta – you will soon return
Back to that land in health and bloom
And then the heath alone will mourn
Above my unremembered tomb
For you'll forget the lonely grave
And mouldering corpse by Elnor's wave' –

A DAY DREAM

On a sunny brae, alone I lay
    One summer afternoon;
It was the marriage-time of May
    With her young lover, June.

From her mother's heart, seemed loath to part
    That queen of bridal charms,
But her father smiled on the fairest child
    He ever held in his arms.

The trees did wave their many crests,
    The glad birds carolled clear;
And I, of all the wedding guests,
    Was only sullen there!

There was not one, but wished to shun
    My aspect void of cheer;
The very grey rocks, looking on,
    Asked, 'What do you here?'

And I could utter no reply;
    In sooth, I did not know
Why I had brought a clouded eye
    To greet the general glow.

So, resting on a heathy bank,
    I took my heart to me;
And we together sadly sank
    Into a reverie.

We thought, 'When winter comes again,
    Where will these bright things be?
All vanished, like a vision vain,
    An unreal mockery!

'The birds that now so blithely sing,
    Through deserts, frozen dry,
Poor spectres of the perished spring,
    In famished troops, will fly.

'And why should we be glad at all?
    The leaf is hardly green,
Before a token of its fall
    Is on the surface seen!'

Now, whether it were really so,
    I never could be sure;
But as in fit of peevish woe,
    I stretched me on the moor,

A thousand thousand gleaming fires
    Seemed kindling in the air;
A thousand thousand silvery lyres
    Resounded far and near:

Methought, the very breath I breathed
    Was full of sparks divine,
And all my heather-couch was wreathed
    By that celestial shine!

And, while the wide earth echoing rung
    To their strange minstrelsy,
The little glittering spirits sung,
    Or seemed to sing, to me.

'O mortal! mortal! let them die;
    Let time and tears destroy,
That we may overflow the sky
    With universal joy!

'Let grief distract the sufferer's breast,
    And night obscure his way;
They hasten him to endless rest,
    And everlasting day.

'To thee the world is like a tomb,
  A desert's naked shore;
To us, in unimagined bloom,
  It brightens more and more!

'And could we lift the veil, and give
  One brief glimpse to thine eye,
Thou wouldst rejoice for those that live,
  Because they live to die.'

The music ceased; the noonday dream,
  Like dream of night, withdrew;
But Fancy, still, will sometimes deem
  Her fond creation true.

THE INSPIRING MUSIC'S
THRILLING SOUND

The inspiring music's thrilling sound
The glory of the festal day
The glittering splendour rising round
Have passed like all earth's joys away

Forsaken by that Lady fair
She glides unheeding through them all
Covering her brow to hide the tear
That still though checked trembling to fall

She hurries through the outer Hall
And up the stairs through galleries dim
That murmur to the breezes' call
The night-wind's lonely vesper hymn

AND FIRST AN HOUR OF
MOURNFUL MUSING

And first an hour of mournful musing
And then a gush of bitter tears
And then a dreary calm diffusing
Its deadly mist o'er joys and cares

And then a throb and then a lightening
And then a breathing from above
And then a star in heaven brightening
The star the glorious star of love

AWAKING MORNING LAUGHS
FROM HEAVEN

Awaking morning laughs from heaven
On golden summer's forests green
And what a gush of song is given
To welcome in that light serene

A fresh wind waves the clustering roses
And through the open window sighs
Around the couch where she reposes
The lady with the dovelike eyes

With dovelike eyes and shining hair
And velvet cheek so sweetly moulded
And hands so soft and white and fair
Above her snowy bosom folded

*

Her sister's and her brother's feet
Are brushing off the scented dew
And she springs up in haste to greet
The grass and flowers and sunshine too

WRITTEN IN ASPIN CASTLE

How do I love on summer nights
To sit within this Norman door
Whose sombre portal hides the lights
Thickening above me evermore!

How do I love to hear the flow
Of Aspin's water murmuring low
And hours long listen to the breeze
That sighs in Rockden's waving trees

Tonight, there is no wind to wake
One ripple on the lonely lake –
Tonight the clouds subdued and grey
Starlight and moonlight shut away

'Tis calm and still and almost drear
So utter is the solitude;
But still I love to linger here
And form my mood to nature's mood –

There's a wild walk beneath the rocks
Following the bend of Aspin's side
'Tis worn by feet of mountain-flocks
That wander down to drink the tide

Never by cliff and gnarled tree
Wound fairy path so sweet to me
Yet of the native shepherds none
In open day and cheerful sun
Will tread its labyrinths alone

Far less when evening's pensive hour
Hushes the bird and shuts the flower
And gives to Fancy magic power
O'er each familiar tone.

For round their h... ... ...they'll tell the tale
And every listener swears it true
How wanders there a phantom pale
With spirit-eyes of dreamy blue—

It always walks with head declined
Its long curls move not in the wind
Its face is fair – divinely fair;

But brooding on that angel brow
Rests such a shade of deep despair
As nought divine could ever know

How oft in twilight lingering lone
I've stood to watch that phantom rise
And seen in mist and moonlit stone
Its gleaming hair and solemn eyes

The ancient men in secret say
'Tis the first chief of Aspin grey
That haunts his feudal home

But why, around that alien grave
Three thousand miles beyond the wave –
Where his exiled ashes lie
Under the cope of England's sky –
Doth he not rather roam?

I've seen his picture in the hall;
It hangs upon an eastern wall
And often when the sun declines
That picture like an angel shines –

And when the moonbeam chill and blue
Streams the spectral windows through
That picture's like a spectre too –

The hall is full of portraits rare;
Beauty and mystery mingle there –
At his right hand an infant fair
Looks from its golden frame –

And just like his its ringlets bright
Its large dark eye of shadowy light
Its cheek's pure hue, its forehead white
And like its noble name –

Daughter divine! and could his gaze
Fall coldly on thy peerless face?
And did he never smile to see
Himself restored to infancy?

Never part back that golden flow
Of curls, and kiss that pearly brow
And feel no other earthly bliss
Was equal to that parent's kiss?

No; turn towards the western side
There stands Sidonia's deity!
In all her glory, all her pride!
And truly like a god she seems
Some god of wild enthusiast's dreams
And this is she for whom he died!
For whom his spirit unforgiven,

Wanders unsheltered shut from heaven
An outcast for eternity –

Those eyes are dust – those lips are clay –
That form is mouldered all away
Nor thought, nor sense, nor pulse, nor breath
The whole devoured and lost in death!

There is no worm, however mean,
That living, is not nobler now
Than she – Lord Alfred's idol queen
So loved – so worshipped long ago –

O come away! the Norman door
Is silvered with a sudden shine –
Come leave these dreams o'er things of yore
And turn to Nature's face divine –

O'er wood and wold, o'er flood and fell
O'er flashing lake and gleaming dell
The harvest moon looks down

And when heaven smiles with love and light
And earth looks back so dazzling bright
In such a scene, on such a night
Earth's children should not frown –

THE OLD CHURCH TOWER
AND GARDEN WALL

The old church tower and garden wall
Are black with Autumn rain
And dreary winds foreboding call
The darkness down again

I watched how evening took the place
Of glad and glorious day
I watched a deeper gloom efface
The evening's lingering ray

And as I gazed on the cheerless sky
Sad thoughts rose in my mind

ALONE I SAT THE SUMMER DAY

Alone I sat the summer day
Had died in smiling light away
I saw it die I watched it fade
From misty hill and breezeless glade

And thoughts in my soul were rushing
And my heart bowed beneath their power
And tears within my eyes were gushing
Because I could not speak the feeling
The solemn joy around me stealing
In that divine untroubled hour

I asked my self O why has heaven
Denied the precious gift to me
The glorious gift to many given
To speak their thoughts in poetry

Dreams have encircled me I said
From careless childhood's sunny time
Visions by ardent fancy fed
Since life was in its morning prime

But now when I had hoped to sing
My fingers strike a tuneless string
And still the burden of the strain
Is strive no more 'tis all in vain

MONTH AFTER MONTH

Month after month year after year
My harp has poured a dreary strain –
At length a livelier note shall cheer
And pleasure tune its chords again

What though the stars and fair moonlight
Are quenched in morning dull and grey
They were but tokens of the night
And *this* my soul is day

EDITOR'S NOTE

Emily Brontë's poems are a reader's pleasure and an editor's headache. Most were unpublished in her lifetime, many appear to be unfinished, punctuation is either erratic or entirely absent, and it is sometimes hard to tell whether the verses are autobiographical, written for the 'Gondal' saga she composed with her sister, Anne, or prompted by other motives.

This edition, which includes most of her surviving poetry, follows recent practice by printing Brontë's own hand as she left it, insofar as her intentions can be determined. Very occasionally, a word clearly required by sense or rhyme has been supplied. And although the obvious 'Gondal' poems are grouped together, I have not tried to impose distinctions between the fictional and the real, the literary and the personal. As readers of *Wuthering Heights* will recognise, the shifting border between fact and dream is a hallmark of this writer's imaginative world.

INDEX OF FIRST LINES